**Harvard
Business
Review**

on

MAKING
SMART
DECISIONS

The Harvard Business Review
paperback series

If you need the best practices and ideas for the business challenges you face—but don't have time to find them—*Harvard Business Review* **paperbacks** are for you. Each book is a collection of HBR's inspiring and useful perspectives on a given management topic, all in one place.

The titles include:

Harvard Business Review on Advancing Your Career

Harvard Business Review on Aligning Technology with Strategy

Harvard Business Review on Building Better Teams

Harvard Business Review on Collaborating Effectively

Harvard Business Review on Communicating Effectively

Harvard Business Review on Finding & Keeping the Best People

Harvard Business Review on Fixing Health Care from Inside & Out

Harvard Business Review on Greening Your Business Profitably

Harvard Business Review on Increasing Customer Loyalty

Harvard Business Review on Inspiring & Executing Innovation

Harvard Business Review on Making Smart Decisions

Harvard Business Review on Managing Supply Chains

Harvard Business Review on Rebuilding Your Business Model

Harvard Business Review on Reinventing Your Marketing

Harvard Business Review on Succeeding As an Entrepreneur

Harvard Business Review on Thriving in Emerging Markets

Harvard Business Review on Winning Negotiations

Harvard Business Review

on

MAKING SMART DECISIONS

Harvard Business Review Press

Boston, Massachusetts

Library of Congress Cataloging-in-Publication Data
Harvard business review on making smart decisions.
    p. cm.—(Harvard business review paperback)
   ISBN 978-1-4221-7239-1 (alk. paper) 1. Decision making.
2. Management. I. Harvard business review.
  HD30.23.H36873 2011
  658.4'03—dc22

                                                   2010054388

Contents

Harvard
Business
Review

on

MAKING
SMART
DECISIONS

The Hidden Traps in Decision Making

by John S. Hammond, Ralph L. Keeney, and Howard Raiffa

MAKING DECISIONS IS THE MOST important job of any executive. It's also the toughest and the riskiest. Bad decisions can damage a business and a career, sometimes irreparably. So where do bad decisions come from? In many cases, they can be traced back to the way the decisions were made—the alternatives were not clearly defined, the right information was not collected, the costs and benefits were not accurately weighed. But sometimes the fault lies not in the decision-making process but rather in the mind of the decision maker. The way the human brain works can sabotage our decisions.

Researchers have been studying the way our minds function in making decisions for half a century. This research, in the laboratory and in the field, has revealed that we use unconscious routines to cope with the complexity inherent in most decisions. These routines, known as *heuristics,* serve us well in most situations. In judging distance, for example, our minds frequently rely on a heuristic that equates clarity with proximity. The clearer an object appears, the closer we judge it to be. The fuzzier it appears, the farther away we assume it must be. This simple mental shortcut helps us to make the continuous stream of distance judgments required to navigate the world.

Yet, like most heuristics, it is not foolproof. On days that are hazier than normal, our eyes will tend to trick our minds into thinking that things are more distant than they actually are. Because the resulting distortion poses few dangers for most of us, we can safely ignore it. For airline pilots, though, the distortion can be catastrophic. That's why pilots are trained to use objective measures of distance in addition to their vision.

Researchers have identified a whole series of such flaws in the way we think in making decisions. Some, like the heuristic for clarity, are sensory misperceptions. Others take the form of biases. Others appear simply as irrational anomalies in our thinking. What makes all these traps so dangerous is their invisibility. Because they are hardwired into our thinking process, we fail to recognize them—even as we fall right into them.

For executives, whose success hinges on the many day-to-day decisions they make or approve, the psychological traps are especially dangerous. They can undermine everything from new-product development to acquisition and divestiture strategy to succession

Idea in Brief

Bad decisions can often be traced back to the way the decisions were made—the alternatives were not clearly defined, the right information was not collected, the costs and benefits were not accurately weighed. But sometimes the fault lies not in the decision-making process but rather in the mind of the decision maker: The way the human brain works can sabotage the choices we make. In this article, first published in 1998, John S. Hammond, Ralph L. Keeney, and Howard Raiffa examine eight psychological traps that can affect the way we make business decisions. The anchoring trap leads us to give disproportionate weight to the first information we receive. The status-quo trap biases us toward maintaining the current situation—even when better alternatives exist. The sunk-cost trap inclines us to perpetuate the mistakes of the past. The confirming-evidence trap leads us to seek out information supporting an existing predilection and to discount opposing information. The framing trap occurs when we misstate a problem, undermining the entire decision-making process. The overconfidence trap makes us overestimate the accuracy of our forecasts. The prudence trap leads us to be overcautious when we make estimates about uncertain events. And the recallability trap prompts us to give undue weight to recent, dramatic events. The best way to avoid all the traps is awareness: forewarned is forearmed. But executives can also take other simple steps to protect themselves and their organizations from these mental lapses to ensure that their important business decisions are sound and reliable.

planning. While no one can rid his or her mind of these ingrained flaws, anyone can follow the lead of airline pilots and learn to understand the traps and compensate for them.

In this article, we examine a number of well-documented psychological traps that are particularly likely to undermine business decisions. In addition to reviewing the causes and manifestations of these traps, we offer some specific ways managers can guard against them. It's important to remember, though, that the best defense is always awareness. Executives who attempt to familiarize themselves with these traps and the diverse forms they take will be better able to ensure that the decisions they make are sound and that the recommendations proposed by subordinates or associates are reliable.

The Anchoring Trap

How would you answer these two questions?

Is the population of Turkey greater than 35 million?

What's your best estimate of Turkey's population?

If you're like most people, the figure of 35 million cited in the first question (a figure we chose arbitrarily) influenced your answer to the second question. Over the years, we've posed those questions to many groups of people. In half the cases, we used 35 million in the first question; in the other half, we used 100 million. Without fail, the answers to the second question increase by many millions when the larger figure is used in the first question. This simple test illustrates the common and often pernicious mental phenomenon known as *anchoring*. When considering a decision, the mind gives disproportionate weight to the first information it receives. Initial impressions, estimates, or data anchor subsequent thoughts and judgments.

Anchors take many guises. They can be as simple and seemingly innocuous as a comment offered by a colleague or a statistic appearing in the morning newspaper. They can be as insidious as a stereotype about a person's skin color, accent, or dress. In business, one of the most common types of anchors is a past event or trend. A marketer attempting to project the sales of a product for the coming year often begins by looking at the sales volumes for past years. The old numbers become anchors, which the forecaster then adjusts based on other factors. This approach, while it may lead to a reasonably accurate estimate, tends to give too much weight to past events and not enough weight to other factors. In situations characterized by rapid changes in the marketplace, historical anchors can lead to poor forecasts and, in turn, misguided choices.

Because anchors can establish the terms on which a decision will be made, they are often used as a bargaining tactic by savvy negotiators. Consider the experience of a large consulting firm that was searching for new office space in San Francisco. Working with a commercial real-estate broker, the firm's partners identified a building that met all their criteria, and they set up a meeting with the building's owners. The owners opened the meeting by laying out the terms of a proposed contract: a ten-year lease; an initial monthly price of $2.50 per square foot; annual price increases at the prevailing inflation rate; all interior improvements to be the tenant's responsibility; an option for the tenant to extend the lease for ten additional years under the same terms. Although the price was at the high end of current market rates, the consultants made a relatively modest counteroffer. They proposed an initial price in the midrange of market rates and asked the owners to share in the renovation expenses, but they accepted all the other terms. The consultants could have been much more aggressive and creative in their counterproposal—reducing the initial price to the low end of market rates, adjusting rates biennially rather than annually, putting a cap on the increases, defining different terms for extending the lease, and so forth— but their thinking was guided by the owners' initial proposal. The consultants had fallen into the anchoring trap, and as a result, they ended up paying a lot more for the space than they had to.

What Can You Do About It?
The effect of anchors in decision making has been documented in thousands of experiments. Anchors influence the decisions not only of managers, but also of accountants and engineers, bankers and lawyers, consultants and stock analysts. No one can avoid their influence; they're just too widespread. But managers who are aware of the dangers of anchors can reduce their impact by using the following techniques:

- Always view a problem from different perspectives. Try using alternative starting points and approaches rather than sticking with the first line of thought that occurs to you.

- Think about the problem on your own before consulting others to avoid becoming anchored by their ideas.

- Be open-minded. Seek information and opinions from a variety of people to widen your frame of reference and to push your mind in fresh directions.

- Be careful to avoid anchoring your advisers, consultants, and others from whom you solicit information and counsel. Tell them as little as possible about your own ideas, estimates, and tentative decisions. If you reveal too much, your own preconceptions may simply come back to you.

- Be particularly wary of anchors in negotiations. Think through your position before any negotiation begins in order to avoid being anchored by the other party's initial proposal. At the same time, look for opportunities to use anchors to your own advantage—if you're the seller, for example, suggest a high, but defensible, price as an opening gambit.

The Status-Quo Trap

We all like to believe that we make decisions rationally and objectively. But the fact is, we all carry biases, and those biases influence the choices we make. Decision makers display, for example, a strong bias toward alternatives that perpetuate the status quo. On a broad scale, we can see this tendency whenever a radically new product is introduced. The first automobiles, revealingly called "horseless carriages," looked very much like the buggies they replaced. The first "electronic newspapers" appearing on the World Wide Web looked very much like their print precursors.

On a more familiar level, you may have succumbed to this bias in your personal financial decisions. People sometimes, for example, inherit shares of stock that they would never have bought themselves. Although it would be a straightforward, inexpensive proposition to sell those shares and put the money into a different investment, a surprising number of people don't sell. They find the status quo comfortable, and they avoid taking action that would upset it. "Maybe I'll rethink it later," they say. But "later" is usually never.

The source of the status-quo trap lies deep within our psyches, in our desire to protect our egos from damage. Breaking from the status quo means taking action, and when we take action, we take responsibility, thus opening ourselves to criticism and to regret. Not surprisingly, we naturally look for reasons to do nothing. Sticking with the status quo represents, in most cases, the safer course because it puts us at less psychological risk.

Many experiments have shown the magnetic attraction of the status quo. In one, a group of people were randomly given one of two gifts of approximately the same value—half received a mug, the other half a Swiss chocolate bar. They were then told that they could easily exchange the gift they received for the other gift. While you might expect that about half would have wanted to make the exchange, only one in ten actually did. The status quo exerted its power even though it had been arbitrarily established only minutes before.

Other experiments have shown that the more choices you are given, the more pull the status quo has. More people will, for instance, choose the status quo when there are two alternatives to it rather than one: A and B instead of just A. Why? Choosing between A and B requires additional effort; selecting the status quo avoids that effort.

In business, where sins of commission (doing something) tend to be punished much more severely than sins of omission (doing nothing), the status quo holds a particularly strong attraction. Many mergers, for example, founder because the acquiring company avoids taking swift action to impose a new, more appropriate management structure on the acquired company. "Let's not rock the boat right now," the typical reasoning goes. "Let's wait until the situation stabilizes." But as time passes, the existing structure becomes more entrenched, and altering it becomes harder, not easier. Having failed to seize the occasion when change would have been expected, management finds itself stuck with the status quo.

What Can You Do About It?

First of all, remember that in any given decision, maintaining the status quo may indeed be the best choice, but you don't want to choose it just because it is comfortable. Once you become aware of the status-quo trap, you can use these techniques to lessen its pull:

- Always remind yourself of your objectives and examine how they would be served by the status quo. You may find that elements of the current situation act as barriers to your goals.

- Never think of the status quo as your only alternative. Identify other options and use them as counterbalances, carefully evaluating all the pluses and minuses.

- Ask yourself whether you would choose the status-quo alternative if, in fact, it weren't the status quo.

- Avoid exaggerating the effort or cost involved in switching from the status quo.

- Remember that the desirability of the status quo will change over time. When comparing alternatives, always evaluate them in terms of the future as well as the present.

- If you have several alternatives that are superior to the status quo, don't default to the status quo just because you're having a hard time picking the best alternative. Force yourself to choose.

The Sunk-Cost Trap

Another of our deep-seated biases is to make choices in a way that justifies past choices, even when the past choices no longer seem valid. Most of us have fallen into this trap. We may have refused, for example, to sell a stock or a mutual fund at a loss, forgoing other, more attractive investments. Or we may have poured enormous effort into improving the performance of an employee whom we knew we shouldn't have hired in the first place. Our past decisions become what economists term *sunk costs*—old investments of time or money that are now irrecoverable. We know, rationally, that sunk costs are irrelevant to the present decision, but nevertheless they prey on our minds, leading us to make inappropriate decisions.

Why can't people free themselves from past decisions? Frequently, it's because they are unwilling, consciously or not, to admit to a mistake. Acknowledging a poor decision in one's personal life may be purely a private matter, involving only one's self-esteem, but in business, a bad decision is often a very public matter, inviting critical comments from colleagues or bosses. If you fire a poor performer whom you hired, you're making a public admission of poor judgment. It seems psychologically safer to let him or her stay on, even though that choice only compounds the error.

The sunk-cost bias shows up with disturbing regularity in banking, where it can have particularly dire consequences. When a borrower's business runs into trouble, a lender will often advance additional funds in hopes of providing the business with some breathing room to recover. If the business does have a good chance of coming back, that's a wise investment. Otherwise, it's just throwing good money after bad.

One of us helped a major U.S. bank recover after it made many bad loans to foreign businesses. We found that the bankers responsible for originating the problem loans were far more likely to advance additional funds—repeatedly, in many cases—than were bankers who took over the accounts after the original loans were made. Too often, the original bankers' strategy—and loans—ended in failure. Having been trapped by an escalation of commitment, they had tried, consciously or unconsciously, to protect their earlier, flawed decisions. They had fallen victim to the sunk-cost bias. The bank finally solved the problem by instituting a policy requiring that a loan be immediately reassigned to another banker as soon as any problem arose. The new banker was able to take a fresh, unbiased look at the merit of offering more funds.

Sometimes a corporate culture reinforces the sunk-cost trap. If the penalties for making a decision that leads to an unfavorable outcome are overly severe, managers will be motivated to let failed projects drag on endlessly—in the vain hope that they'll somehow be able to transform them into successes. Executives should recognize that, in an uncertain world where unforeseeable events are common, good decisions can sometimes lead to bad outcomes. By acknowledging that some good ideas will end in failure, executives will encourage people to cut their losses rather than let them mount.

What Can You Do About It?

For all decisions with a history, you will need to make a conscious effort to set aside any sunk costs—whether psychological or economic—that will muddy your thinking about the choice at hand. Try these techniques:

- Seek out and listen carefully to the views of people who were uninvolved with the earlier decisions and who are hence unlikely to be committed to them.

- Examine why admitting to an earlier mistake distresses you. If the problem lies in your own wounded self-esteem, deal with it head-on. Remind yourself that even smart choices can have bad consequences, through no fault of the original decision maker, and that even the best and most experienced managers are not immune to errors in judgment. Remember the wise words of Warren Buffett: "When you find yourself in a hole, the best thing you can do is stop digging."

- Be on the lookout for the influence of sunk-cost biases in the decisions and recommendations made by your subordinates. Reassign responsibilities when necessary.

- Don't cultivate a failure-fearing culture that leads employees to perpetuate their mistakes. In rewarding people, look at the quality of their decision making (taking into account what was known at the time their decisions were made), not just the quality of the outcomes.

The Confirming-Evidence Trap

Imagine that you're the president of a successful mid-size U.S. manufacturer considering whether to call off a planned plant expansion. For a while you've been concerned that your company won't be able to sustain the rapid pace of growth of its exports. You fear that the value of the U.S. dollar will strengthen in coming months, making your goods more costly for overseas consumers and dampening demand. But before you put the brakes on the plant expansion, you decide to call up an acquaintance, the chief executive of a similar company that recently mothballed a new factory, to check her reasoning. She presents a strong case that other currencies are about to weaken significantly against the dollar. What do you do?

You'd better not let that conversation be the clincher, because you've probably just fallen victim to the confirming-evidence bias. This bias leads us to seek out information that supports our existing instinct or point of view while avoiding information that contradicts it. What, after all, did you expect your acquaintance to give, other than a strong argument in favor of her own decision? The confirming-evidence bias not only affects where we go to collect evidence but also how we interpret the evidence we do receive, leading us to give too much weight to supporting information and too little to conflicting information.

In one psychological study of this phenomenon, two groups—one opposed to and one supporting capital punishment—each read two reports of carefully conducted research on the effectiveness of the death penalty as a deterrent to crime. One report concluded that the death penalty was effective; the other concluded it was not. Despite being exposed to solid scientific information supporting counterarguments, the members of both groups became even more convinced of the validity of their own position after reading both reports. They automatically accepted the supporting information and dismissed the conflicting information.

There are two fundamental psychological forces at work here. The first is our tendency to subconsciously decide what we want to do before we figure out why we want to do it. The second is our inclination to be more engaged by things we like than by things we dislike—a tendency well documented even in babies. Naturally, then, we are drawn to information that supports our subconscious leanings.

What Can You Do About It?

It's not that you shouldn't make the choice you're subconsciously drawn to. It's just that you want to be sure it's the smart choice. You need to put it to the test. Here's how:

- Always check to see whether you are examining all the evidence with equal rigor. Avoid the tendency to accept confirming evidence without question.

- Get someone you respect to play devil's advocate, to argue against the decision you're contemplating. Better yet, build the counterarguments yourself. What's the strongest reason to do something else? The second strongest reason? The third? Consider the position with an open mind.

- Be honest with yourself about your motives. Are you really gathering information to help you make a smart choice, or are you just looking for evidence confirming what you think you'd like to do?

- In seeking the advice of others, don't ask leading questions that invite confirming evidence. And if you find that an adviser always seems to support your point of view, find a new adviser. Don't surround yourself with yes-men.

The Framing Trap

The first step in making a decision is to frame the question. It's also one of the most dangerous steps. The way a problem is framed can profoundly influence the choices you make. In a case involving automobile insurance, for example, framing made a $200 million difference. To reduce insurance costs, two neighboring states, New Jersey and Pennsylvania, made similar changes in their laws. Each state gave drivers a new option: By accepting a limited right to sue, they could lower their premiums. But the two states framed the choice in very different ways: In New Jersey, you automatically got the limited right to sue unless you specified otherwise; in Pennsylvania, you got the full right to sue unless you specified otherwise. The different frames established different status quos, and, not surprisingly, most consumers defaulted to the status quo. As a result, in New Jersey about 80% of drivers chose the limited right to sue, but in Pennsylvania only 25% chose it. Because of the way it framed the choice, Pennsylvania failed to gain approximately $200 million in expected insurance and litigation savings.

The framing trap can take many forms, and as the insurance example shows, it is often closely related to other psychological traps. A frame can establish the status quo or introduce an anchor. It can highlight sunk costs or lead you toward confirming evidence. Decision researchers have documented two types of frames that distort decision making with particular frequency.

Frames as Gains Versus Losses
In a study patterned after a classic experiment by decision researchers Daniel Kahneman and Amos Tversky, one of us posed the following problem to a group of insurance professionals:

> You are a marine property adjuster charged with minimizing the loss of cargo on three insured barges that sank yesterday off the coast of Alaska. Each barge holds $200,000 worth of cargo, which will be lost if not salvaged within 72 hours. The owner of a local marine-salvage company gives you two options, both of which will cost the same:
> **Plan A:** This plan will save the cargo of one of the three barges, worth $200,000.
> **Plan B:** This plan has a one-third probability of saving the cargo on all three barges, worth $600,000, but has a two-thirds probability of saving nothing.
> Which plan would you choose?

If you are like 71% of the respondents in the study, you chose the "less risky" Plan A, which will save one barge for sure. Another group in the study, however, was asked to choose between alternatives C and D:

> **Plan C:** This plan will result in the loss of two of the three cargoes, worth $400,000.

Plan D: This plan has a two-thirds probability of resulting in the loss of all three cargoes and the entire $600,000 but has a one-third probability of losing no cargo.

Faced with this choice, 80% of these respondents preferred Plan D.

The pairs of alternatives are, of course, precisely equivalent—Plan A is the same as Plan C, and Plan B is the same as Plan D—they've just been framed in different ways. The strikingly different responses reveal that people are risk averse when a problem is posed in terms of gains (barges saved) but risk seeking when a problem is posed in terms of avoiding losses (barges lost). Furthermore, they tend to adopt the frame as it is presented to them rather than restating the problem in their own way.

Framing with different reference points

The same problem can also elicit very different responses when frames use different reference points. Let's say you have $2,000 in your checking account and you are asked the following question:

Would you accept a fifty-fifty chance of either losing $300 or winning $500?

Would you accept the chance? What if you were asked this question:

Would you prefer to keep your checking account balance of $2,000 or to accept a fifty-fifty chance of having either $1,700 or $2,500 in your account?

Once again, the two questions pose the same problem. While your answers to both questions should, rationally speaking, be the same, studies have shown that many people would refuse the fifty-fifty chance in the first question but accept it in the second. Their different reactions result from the different reference points presented in the two frames. The first frame, with its reference point of zero, emphasizes incremental gains and losses, and the thought of losing triggers a conservative response in many people's minds. The second frame, with its reference point of $2,000, puts things into perspective by emphasizing the real financial impact of the decision.

What Can You Do About It?

A poorly framed problem can undermine even the best-considered decision. But any adverse effect of framing can be limited by taking the following precautions:

- Don't automatically accept the initial frame, whether it was formulated by you or by someone else. Always try to reframe the problem in various ways. Look for distortions caused by the frames.

- Try posing problems in a neutral, redundant way that combines gains and losses or embraces different reference points. For example: Would you accept a fifty-fifty chance of either losing $300, resulting in a bank balance of $1,700, or winning $500, resulting in a bank balance of $2,500?

- Think hard throughout your decision-making process about the framing of the problem. At points throughout the process, particularly near the end, ask yourself how your thinking might change if the framing changed.

- When others recommend decisions, examine the way they framed the problem. Challenge them with different frames.

The Estimating and Forecasting Traps

Most of us are adept at making estimates about time, distance, weight, and volume. That's because we're constantly making judgments about these variables and getting quick feedback about the accuracy of those judgments. Through daily practice, our minds become finely calibrated.

Making estimates or forecasts about uncertain events, however, is a different matter. While managers continually make such estimates and forecasts, they rarely get clear feedback about their accuracy. If you judge, for example, that the likelihood of the price of oil falling to less than $15 a barrel one year hence is about 40% and the price does indeed fall to that level, you can't tell whether you were right or wrong about the probability you estimated. The only way to gauge your accuracy would be to keep track of many, many similar judgments to see if, after the fact, the events you thought had a 40% chance of occurring actually did occur 40% of the time. That would require a great deal of data, carefully tracked over a long period of time. Weather forecasters and book-makers have the opportunities and incentives to maintain such records, but the rest of us don't. As a result, our minds never become calibrated for making estimates in the face of uncertainty.

All of the traps we've discussed so far can influence the way we make decisions when confronted with uncertainty. But there's another set of traps that can have a particularly distorting effect in uncertain situations because they cloud our ability to assess probabilities. Let's look at three of the most common of these uncertainty traps.

The Overconfidence Trap

Even though most of us are not very good at making estimates or forecasts, we actually tend to be overconfident about our accuracy. That can lead to errors in judgment and, in turn, bad decisions. In one series of tests, people were asked to forecast the next week's closing value for the Dow Jones Industrial Average. To account for uncertainty, they were then asked to estimate a range within which the closing value would likely fall. In picking the top number of the range, they were asked to choose a high estimate they thought had only a 1% chance of being exceeded by the closing value. Similarly, for the bottom end, they were told to pick a low estimate for which they thought there would be only a 1% chance of the closing value falling below it. If they were good at judging their forecasting accuracy, you'd expect the participants to be wrong only about 2% of the time. But hundreds of tests have shown that the actual Dow Jones averages fell outside the forecast ranges 20% to 30% of the time. Overly confident about the accuracy of their predictions, most people set too narrow a range of possibilities.

Think of the implications for business decisions, in which major initiatives and investments often hinge on ranges of estimates. If managers underestimate the high end or overestimate the low end of a crucial variable, they may miss attractive opportunities or expose themselves to far greater risk than they realize. Much money has been wasted on ill-fated product-development projects because managers did not accurately account for the possibility of market failure.

The Prudence Trap

Another trap for forecasters takes the form of overcautiousness, or prudence. When faced with high-stakes decisions, we tend to adjust our estimates or forecasts "just to be on the safe side." Many years ago, for example, one of the Big Three U.S. automakers was deciding how many of a new-model car to produce in anticipation of its busiest sales season. The market-planning department, responsible for the decision, asked other departments to supply forecasts of key variables such as anticipated sales, dealer inventories, competitor actions, and costs. Knowing the purpose of the estimates, each department slanted its forecast to favor building more cars—"just to be safe." But the market planners took the numbers at face value and then made their own "just to be safe" adjustments. Not surprisingly, the number of cars produced far exceeded demand, and the company took six months to sell off the surplus, resorting in the end to promotional pricing.

Policy makers have gone so far as to codify overcautiousness in formal decision procedures. An extreme example is the methodology of "worst-case analysis," which was once popular in the design of weapons systems and is still used in certain engineering and regulatory settings. Using this approach, engineers designed weapons to operate under the worst possible combination of circumstances, even though the odds of those circumstances actually coming to pass were infinitesimal. Worst-case analysis added enormous costs with no practical benefit (in fact, it often backfired by touching off an arms race), proving that too much prudence can sometimes be as dangerous as too little.

The Recallability Trap

Even if we are neither overly confident nor unduly prudent, we can still fall into a trap when making estimates or forecasts. Because we frequently base our predictions about future events on our memory of past events, we can be overly influenced by dramatic events—those that leave a strong impression on our memory. We all, for example, exaggerate the probability of rare but catastrophic occurrences such as plane crashes because they get disproportionate attention in the media. A dramatic or traumatic event in your own life can also distort your thinking. You will assign a higher probability to traffic accidents if you have passed one on the way to work, and you will assign a higher chance of someday dying of cancer yourself if a close friend has died of the disease.

In fact, anything that distorts your ability to recall events in a balanced way will distort your probability assessments. In one experiment, lists of well-known men and women were read to different groups of people. Unbeknownst to the subjects, each list had an equal number of men and women, but on some lists the men were more famous than the women while on others the women were more famous. Afterward, the participants were asked to estimate the percentages of men and women on each list. Those who had heard the list with the more famous men thought there were more men on the list, while those who had heard the one with the more famous women thought there were more women.

Corporate lawyers often get caught in the recallability trap when defending liability suits. Their decisions about whether to settle a claim or take it to court usually hinge on their assessments of the possible outcomes of a trial. Because the media tend to aggressively publicize massive damage awards (while ignoring other, far more common trial outcomes), lawyers can overestimate the probability of a large award for the plaintiff. As a result, they offer larger settlements than are actually warranted.

What Can You Do About It?

The best way to avoid the estimating and forecasting traps is to take a very disciplined approach to making forecasts and judging probabilities. For each of the three traps, some additional precautions can be taken:

- To reduce the effects of overconfidence in making estimates, always start by considering the extremes, the low and high ends of the possible range of values. This will help you avoid being anchored by an initial estimate. Then challenge your estimates of the extremes. Try to imagine circumstances where the actual figure would fall below your low or above your high, and adjust your range accordingly. Challenge the estimates of your subordinates and advisers in a similar fashion. They're also susceptible to overconfidence.

- To avoid the prudence trap, always state your estimates honestly and explain to anyone who will be using them that they have not been adjusted. Emphasize the need for honest input to anyone who will be supplying you with estimates. Test estimates over a reasonable range to assess their impact. Take a second look at the more sensitive estimates.

- To minimize the distortion caused by variations in recallability, carefully examine all your assumptions to ensure they're not unduly influenced by your memory. Get actual statistics whenever possible. Try not to be guided by impressions.

Forewarned Is Forearmed

When it comes to business decisions, there's rarely such a thing as a no-brainer. Our brains are always at work, sometimes, unfortunately, in ways that hinder rather than help us. At every stage of the decision-making process, misperceptions, biases, and other tricks of the mind can influence the choices we make. Highly complex and important decisions are the most prone to distortion because they tend to involve the most assumptions, the most estimates, and the most inputs from the most people. The higher the stakes, the higher the risk of being caught in a psychological trap.

The traps we've reviewed can all work in isolation. But, even more dangerous, they can work in concert, amplifying one another. A dramatic first impression might anchor our thinking, and then we might selectively seek out confirming evidence to justify our initial inclination. We make a hasty decision, and that decision establishes a new status quo. As our sunk costs mount, we become trapped, unable to find a propitious time to seek out a new and possibly better course. The psychological miscues cascade, making it harder and harder to choose wisely.

As we said at the outset, the best protection against all psychological traps—in isolation or in combination—is awareness. Forewarned is forearmed. Even if you can't eradicate the distortions ingrained into the way your mind works, you can build tests and disciplines into your decision-making process that can uncover errors in thinking before they become errors in judgment. And taking action to understand and avoid psychological traps can have the added benefit of increasing your confidence in the choices you make.

JOHN S. HAMMOND is a consultant on decision making and a former Harvard Business School professor. **RALPH L. KEENEY** is a professor at Duke University's Fuqua School of Business. **HOWARD RAIFFA** is the Frank Plumpton Ramsey Professor of Managerial Economics, Emeritus, at Harvard Business School.

Originally published in January 2006. Reprint R0601K

Delusions of Success

How Optimism Undermines Executives'
Decisions
by Dan Lovallo and Daniel Kahneman

IN 1992, OXFORD HEALTH PLANS started to build a complex new computer system for processing claims and payments. From the start, the project was hampered by unforeseen problems and delays. As the company fell further behind schedule and budget, it struggled, vainly, to stem an ever rising flood of paperwork. When, on October 27, 1997, Oxford disclosed that its system and its accounts were in disarray, the company's stock price dropped 63%, destroying more than $3 billion in shareholder value in a single day.

Early in the 1980s, the United Kingdom, Germany, Italy, and Spain announced that they would work together to build the Eurofighter, an advanced military jet. The project was expected to cost $20 billion, and the jet was slated to go into service in 1997. Today, after nearly two decades of technical glitches and unexpected expenses, the aircraft has yet to be deployed, and projected costs have more than doubled, to approximately $45 billion.

In 1996, the Union Pacific railroad bought its competitor Southern Pacific for $3.9 billion, creating the largest rail carrier in North America. Almost immediately, the two companies began to have serious difficulties merging their operations, leading to snarled traffic, lost cargo, and massive delays. As the situation got worse, and the company's stock price tumbled, customers and shareholders sued the railroad, and it had to cut its dividend and raise new capital to address the problems.

Debacles like these are all too common in business. Most large capital investment projects come in late and over budget, never living up to expectations. More than 70% of new manufacturing plants in North America, for example, close within their first decade of operation. Approximately three-quarters of mergers and acquisitions never pay off—the acquiring firm's shareholders lose more than the acquired firm's shareholders gain. And efforts to enter new markets fare no better; the vast majority end up being abandoned within a few years.

According to standard economic theory, the high failure rates are simple to explain: The frequency of poor outcomes is an unavoidable result of companies taking rational risks in uncertain situations. Entrepreneurs and managers know and accept the odds because the rewards of success are sufficiently enticing. In the long run, the gains from a few successes will outweigh the losses from many failures.

Idea in Brief

The evidence is disturbingly clear: Most major business initiatives—mergers and acquisitions, capital investments, market entries—fail to pay off. Economists would argue that the low success rate reflects a rational assessment of risk, with the returns from a few successes outweighing the losses of many failures. But two distinguished scholars of decision making, Dan Lovallo of the University of New South Wales and Nobel laureate Daniel Kahneman of Princeton University, provide a very different explanation. They show that a combination of cognitive biases (including anchoring and competitor neglect) and organizational pressures lead managers to make overly optimistic forecasts in analyzing proposals for major investments. By exaggerating the likely benefits of a project and ignoring the potential pitfalls, they lead their organizations into initiatives that are doomed to fall well short of expectations. The biases and pressures cannot be escaped, the authors argue, but they can be tempered by applying a very different method of forecasting—one that takes a much more objective "outside view" of an initiative's likely outcome. This outside view, also known as reference-class forecasting, completely ignores the details of the project at hand; instead, it encourages managers to examine the experiences of a class of similar projects, to lay out a rough distribution of outcomes for this reference class, and then to position the current project in that distribution.

This is, to be sure, an attractive argument from the perspective of executives. It effectively relieves them of blame for failed projects—after all, they were just taking reasonable risks. But having examined this phenomenon from two very different points of view—a business scholar's and a psychologist's—we have come to a different conclusion. We don't believe that the high number of business failures is best explained as the result of rational choices gone wrong. Rather, we see it as a consequence of flawed decision making.

When forecasting the outcomes of risky projects, executives all too easily fall victim to what psychologists call the planning fallacy. In its grip, managers make decisions based on delusional optimism rather than on a rational weighting of gains, losses, and probabilities. They overestimate benefits and underestimate costs. They spin scenarios of success while overlooking the potential for mistakes and miscalculations. As a result, managers pursue initiatives that are unlikely to come in on budget or on time—or to ever deliver the expected returns.

Executives' overoptimism can be traced both to cognitive biases—to errors in the way the mind processes information—and to organizational pressures. These biases and pressures are ubiquitous, but their effects can be tempered. By supplementing traditional forecasting processes, which tend to focus on a company's own capabilities, experiences, and expectations, with a simple statistical analysis of analogous efforts completed earlier, executives can gain a much more accurate understanding of a project's likely outcome. Such an *outside view,* as we call it, provides a reality check on the more intuitive *inside view,* reducing the odds that a company will rush blindly into a disastrous investment of money and time.

Rose-Colored Glasses

Most people are highly optimistic most of the time. Research into human cognition has traced this overoptimism to many sources. One of the most powerful is the tendency of individuals to exaggerate their own talents—to believe they are above average in their endowment of positive traits and abilities. Consider a survey of 1 million students conducted by the College Board in the 1970s. When asked to rate themselves in comparison to their peers, 70% of the students said they were above average in leadership ability, while only 2% rated themselves below average. For athletic prowess, 60% saw themselves above the median, 6% below. When assessing their ability to get along with others, 60% of the students judged themselves to be in the top decile, and fully 25% considered themselves to be in the top 1%.

The inclination to exaggerate our talents is amplified by our tendency to misperceive the causes of certain events. The typical pattern of such attribution errors, as psychologists call them, is for people to take credit for positive outcomes and to attribute negative outcomes to external factors, no matter what their true cause. One study of letters to shareholders in annual reports, for example, found that executives tend to attribute favorable outcomes to factors under their control, such as their corporate strategy or their R&D programs. Unfavorable outcomes, by contrast, were more likely to be attributed to uncontrollable external factors such as weather or inflation. Similar self-serving attributions have been found in other studies of annual reports and executive speeches.

We also tend to exaggerate the degree of control we have over events, discounting the role of luck. In one series of studies, participants were asked to press a button that could illuminate a red light. The people were told that whether the light flashed was determined by a combination of their action and random chance. Afterward, they were asked to assess what they experienced. Most people grossly overstated the influence of their action in determining whether the light flashed.

Executives and entrepreneurs seem to be highly susceptible to these biases. Studies that compare the actual outcomes of capital investment projects, mergers and acquisitions, and market entries with managers' original expectations for those ventures show a strong tendency toward overoptimism. An analysis of start-up ventures in a wide range of industries found, for example, that more than 80% failed to achieve their market-share target. The studies are backed up by observations of executives. Like other people, business leaders routinely exaggerate their personal abilities, particularly for ambiguous, hard-to-measure traits like managerial skill. Their self-confidence can lead them to assume that they'll be able to avoid or easily overcome potential problems in executing a project. This misapprehension is further exaggerated by managers' tendency to take personal credit for lucky breaks. Think of mergers and acquisitions, for instance. Mergers tend to come in waves, during periods of economic expansion. At such times, executives can overattribute their company's strong performance to their own actions and abilities rather than to the buoyant economy. This can, in turn, lead them to an inflated belief in their own talents. Consequently, many M&A decisions may be the result of hubris, as the executives evaluating an acquisition candidate come to believe that, with proper planning and superior management skills, they could make it more valuable. Research on postmerger performance suggests that, on average, they are mistaken.

Managers are also prone to the illusion that they are in control. Sometimes, in fact, they will explicitly deny the role of chance in the outcome of their plans. They see risk as a challenge to be met by the exercise of skill, and they believe results are determined purely by their own actions and those of their organizations. In their idealized self-image, these executives are not gamblers but prudent and determined agents, who are in control of both people and events. When it comes to making forecasts, therefore, they tend to ignore or downplay the possibility of random or uncontrollable occurrences that may impede their progress toward a goal.

The cognitive biases that produce overoptimism are compounded by the limits of human imagination. No matter how detailed, the business scenarios used in planning are generally inadequate. The reason is simple: Any complex project is subject to myriad problems—from technology failures to shifts in exchange rates to bad weather—and it is beyond the reach of the human imagination to foresee all of them at the outset. As a result, scenario planning can seriously understate the probability of things going awry. Often, for instance, managers will establish a "most likely" scenario and then assume that its outcome is in fact the most likely outcome. But that assumption can be wrong. Because the managers have not fully considered all the possible sequences of events that might delay or otherwise disrupt the project, they are likely to understate the overall probability of unfavorable outcomes. Even though any one of those outcomes may have only a small chance of occurring, in combination they may actually be far more likely to happen than the so-called most likely scenario.

Accentuating the Positive

In business situations, people's native optimism is further magnified by two other kinds of cognitive bias—anchoring and competitor neglect—as well as political pressures to emphasize the positive and downplay the negative. Let's look briefly at each of these three phenomena.

Anchoring

When executives and their subordinates make forecasts about a project, they typically have, as a starting point, a preliminary plan drawn up by the person or team proposing the initiative. They adjust this original plan based on market research, financial analysis, or their own professional judgment before arriving at decisions about whether and how to proceed. This intuitive and seemingly unobjectionable process has serious pitfalls, however. Because the initial plan will tend to accentuate the positive—as a proposal, it's designed to make the case for the project—it will skew the subsequent analysis toward overoptimism. This phenomenon is the result of anchoring, one of the strongest and most prevalent of cognitive biases.

In one experiment that revealed the power of anchoring, people were asked for the last four digits of their Social Security number. They were then asked whether the number of physicians in Manhattan is larger or smaller than the number formed by those four digits. Finally, they were asked to estimate what the number of Manhattan physicians actually is. The correlation between the Social Security number and the estimate was significantly positive. The subjects started from a random series of digits and then insufficiently adjusted their estimate away from it.

Anchoring can be especially pernicious when it comes to forecasting the cost of major capital projects. When executives set budgets for such initiatives, they build in contingency funds to cover overruns. Often, however, they fail to put in enough. That's because they're anchored to their original cost estimates and don't adjust them sufficiently to account for the likelihood of problems and delays, not to mention expansions in the scope of the projects. One Rand Corporation study of 44 chemical-processing plants owned by major companies like 3M, DuPont, and Texaco found that, on average, the factories' actual construction costs were more than double the initial estimates. Furthermore, even a year after start-up, about half the plants produced at less than 75% of their design capacity, with a quarter producing at less than 50%. Many of the plants had their performance expectations permanently lowered, and the owners never realized a return on their investments.

Competitor Neglect

One of the key factors influencing the outcome of a business initiative is competitors' behavior. In making forecasts, however, executives tend to focus on their own company's capabilities and plans and are thus prone to neglect the potential abilities and actions of rivals. Here, again, the result is an underestimation of the potential for negative events—in this case, price wars, overcapacity, and the like. Joe Roth, the former chairman of Walt Disney Studios, expressed the problem well in a 1996 interview with the *Los Angeles Times*: "If you only think about your own business, you think, 'I've got a good story department, I've got a good marketing department, we're going to go out and do this.' And you don't think that everybody else is thinking the same way."

Neglecting competitors can be particularly destructive in efforts to enter new markets. When a company identifies a rapidly growing market well suited to its products and capabilities, it will often rush to gain a beachhead in it, investing heavily in production capacity and marketing. The effort is often justified by the creation of attractive pro forma forecasts of financial results. But such forecasts rarely account for the fact that many other competitors will also target the market, convinced that they, too, have what it takes to succeed. As all these companies invest, supply outstrips demand, quickly rendering the new market unprofitable. Even savvy venture capitalists fell into this trap during the recent ill-fated Internet boom.

Organizational Pressure

Every company has only a limited amount of money and time to devote to new projects. Competition for this time and money is intense, as individuals and units jockey to present their own proposals as being the most attractive for investment. Because forecasts are critical weapons in these battles, individuals and units have big incentives to accentuate the positive in laying out prospective outcomes. This has two ill effects. First, it ensures that the forecasts used for planning are overoptimistic, which, as we described in our discussion of anchoring, distorts all further analysis. Second, it raises the odds that the projects chosen for investment will be those with the most overoptimistic forecasts—and hence the highest probability of disappointment.

Other organizational practices also encourage optimism. Senior executives tend, for instance, to stress the importance of stretch goals for their business units. This can have the salutary effect of increasing motivation, but it can also lead unit managers to further skew their forecasts toward unrealistically rosy outcomes. (And when these forecasts become the basis for compensation targets, the practice can push employees to behave in dangerously risky ways.) Organizations also actively discourage pessimism, which is often interpreted as disloyalty. The bearers of bad news tend to become pariahs, shunned and ignored by other employees. When pessimistic opinions are suppressed, while optimistic ones are rewarded, an organization's ability to think critically is undermined. The optimistic

biases of individual employees become mutually rein-
forcing, and unrealistic views of the future are vali-
dated by the group.

The Outside View

For most of us, the tendency toward optimism is unavoidable. And it's unlikely that companies can, or
would even want to, remove the organizational pressures that promote optimism. Still, optimism can, and
should, be tempered. Simply understanding the sources
of overoptimism can help planners challenge assumptions, bring in alternative perspectives, and in general
take a balanced view of the future.

But there's also a more formal way to improve the reliability of forecasts. Companies can introduce into
their planning processes an objective forecasting
method that counteracts the personal and organizational sources of optimism. We'll begin our exploration
of this approach with an anecdote that illustrates both
the traditional mode of forecasting and the suggested
alternative.

In 1976, one of us was involved in a project to develop
a curriculum for a new subject area for high schools in
Israel. The project was conducted by a small team of
academics and teachers. When the team had been operating for about a year and had some significant achieve-
ments under its belt, its discussions turned to the
question of how long the project would take. Everyone
on the team was asked to write on a slip of paper
the number of months that would be needed to finish

the project—defined as having a complete report ready for submission to the Ministry of Education. The estimates ranged from 18 to 30 months.

One of the team members—a distinguished expert in curriculum development—was then posed a challenge by another team member: "Surely, we're not the only team to have tried to develop a curriculum where none existed before. Try to recall as many such projects as you can. Think of them as they were in a stage comparable to ours at present. How long did it take them at that point to reach completion?" After a long silence, the curriculum expert said, with some discomfort, "First, I should say that not all the teams that I can think of, that were at a comparable stage, ever did complete their task. About 40% of them eventually gave up. Of the remaining, I cannot think of any that completed their task in less than seven years, nor of any that took more than ten." He was then asked if he had reason to believe that the present team was more skilled in curriculum development than the earlier ones had been. "No," he replied, "I cannot think of any relevant factor that distinguishes us favorably from the teams I have been thinking about. Indeed, my impression is that we are slightly below average in terms of resources and potential." The wise decision at this point would probably have been for the team to disband. Instead, the members ignored the pessimistic information and proceeded with the project. They finally completed the initiative eight years later, and their efforts went largely for naught—the resulting curriculum was rarely used.

In this example, the curriculum expert made two forecasts for the same problem and arrived at very different answers. We call these two distinct modes of forecasting the inside view and the outside view. The inside view is the one that the expert and all the other team members spontaneously adopted. They made forecasts by focusing tightly on the case at hand—considering its objective, the resources they brought to it, and the obstacles to its completion; constructing in their minds scenarios of their coming progress; and extrapolating current trends into the future. Not surprisingly, the resulting forecasts, even the most conservative ones, were exceedingly optimistic.

The outside view, also known as reference-class forecasting, is the one that the curriculum expert was encouraged to adopt. It completely ignored the details of the project at hand, and it involved no attempt at forecasting the events that would influence the project's future course. Instead, it examined the experiences of a class of similar projects, laid out a rough distribution of outcomes for this reference class, and then positioned the current project in that distribution. The resulting forecast, as it turned out, was much more accurate.

The contrast between inside and outside views has been confirmed in systematic research. Recent studies have shown that when people are asked simple questions requiring them to take an outside view, their forecasts become significantly more objective and reliable. For example, a group of students enrolling at a college were asked to rate their future academic performance relative to their peers in their major. On average, these students expected to perform better than 84% of their peers, which is logically impossible. Another group of incoming students from the same major were asked about their entrance scores and their peers' scores before being asked about their expected performance. This simple detour into pertinent outside-view information, which both groups of subjects were aware of, reduced the second group's average expected performance ratings by 20%. That's still overconfident, but it's much more realistic than the forecast made by the first group.

Most individuals and organizations are inclined to adopt the inside view in planning major initiatives. It's not only the traditional approach; it's also the intuitive one. The natural way to think about a complex project is to focus on the project itself—to bring to bear all one knows about it, paying special attention to its unique or unusual features. The thought of going out and gathering statistics about related cases seldom enters a planner's mind. The curriculum expert, for example, did not take the outside view until prompted—even though he already had all the information he needed. Even when companies bring in independent consultants to assist in forecasting, they often remain stuck in the inside view. If the consultants provide comparative data on other companies or projects, they can spur useful outside-view thinking. But if they concentrate on the project itself, their analysis will also tend to be distorted by cognitive biases.

While understandable, managers' preference for the inside view over the outside view is unfortunate. When both forecasting methods are applied with equal intelligence and skill, the outside view is much more likely to yield a realistic estimate. That's because it bypasses cognitive and organizational biases. In the outside view, managers aren't required to weave scenarios, imagine events, or gauge their own levels of ability and control—so they can't get all those things wrong. And it doesn't matter if managers aren't good at assessing competitors' abilities and actions; the impact of those abilities and actions is already reflected in the outcomes of the earlier projects within the reference class. It's true that the outside view, being based on historical precedent, may fail to predict extreme outcomes— those that lie outside all historical precedents. But for most projects, the outside view will produce superior results.

The outside view's advantage is most pronounced for initiatives that companies have never attempted before—like building a plant with a new manufacturing technology or entering an entirely new market. It is in the planning of such de novo efforts that the biases toward optimism are likely to be great. Ironically, however, such cases are precisely where the organizational and personal pressures to apply the inside view are most intense. Managers feel that if they don't fully account for the intricacies of the proposed project, they would be derelict in their duties. Indeed, the preference for the inside view over the outside view can feel almost like a moral imperative. The inside view is embraced as a serious attempt to come to grips with the complexities of a unique challenge, while the outside view is rejected as relying on a crude analogy to superficially similar instances. Yet the fact remains: The outside view is more likely to produce accurate forecasts and much less likely to deliver highly unrealistic ones.

Of course, choosing the right class of analogous cases becomes more difficult when executives are forecasting initiatives for which precedents are not easily found. It's not like in the curriculum example, where many similar efforts had already been undertaken. Imagine that planners have to forecast the results of an investment in a new and unfamiliar technology. Should they look at their company's earlier investments in new technologies? Or should they look at how other companies carried out projects involving similar technologies? Neither is perfect, but each will provide useful insights—so the planners should analyze both sets of analogous cases. We provide a fuller explanation of how to identify and analyze a reference class in the sidebar "How to Take the Outside View."

Putting Optimism in Its Place

We are not suggesting that optimism is bad, or that managers should try to root it out of themselves or their organizations. Optimism generates much more enthusiasm than does realism (not to mention pessimism), and it enables people to be resilient when confronting difficult situations or challenging goals. Companies have to promote optimism to keep employees motivated and focused. At the same time, though, they have to generate realistic forecasts, especially when large

How to Take the Outside View

MAKING A FORECAST USING THE outside view requires planners to identify a reference class of analogous past initiatives, determine the distribution of outcomes for those initiatives, and place the project at hand at an appropriate point along that distribution. This effort is best organized into five steps:[1]

1. Select a reference class. Identifying the right reference class involves both art and science. You usually have to weigh similarities and differences on many variables and determine which are the most meaningful in judging how your own initiative will play out. Sometimes that's easy. If you're a studio executive trying to forecast sales of a new film, you'll formulate a reference class based on recent films in the same genre, starring similar actors, with comparable budgets, and so on. In other cases, it's much trickier. If you're a manager at a chemical company that is considering building an olefin plant incorporating a new processing technology, you may instinctively think that your reference class would include olefin plants now in operation. But you may actually get better results by looking at other chemical plants built with new processing technologies. The plant's outcome, in other words, may be more influenced by the newness of its technology than by what it produces. In forecasting an outcome in a competitive situation, such as the market share for a new venture, you need to consider industrial structure and market factors in designing a reference class. The key is to choose a class that is broad enough to be statistically meaningful but narrow enough to be truly comparable to the project at hand.

2. Assess the distribution of outcomes. Once the reference class is chosen, you have to document the outcomes of the prior projects and arrange them as a distribution, showing the extremes, the median, and any clusters. Sometimes you won't be able to precisely document the outcomes of every member of the class. But you can still arrive at a rough distribution by calculating the average outcome as well as a measure of variability. In the film example, for instance, you may find that the reference-class movies sold $40 million worth of tickets on average, but that 10% sold less than $2 million worth of tickets and 5% sold more than $120 million worth.

3. Make an intuitive prediction of your project's position in the distribution. Based on your own understanding of the project at hand and how it compares with the projects in the reference class, predict where it would fall along the distribution. Because your intuitive estimate will likely be biased, the final two steps are intended to adjust the estimate in order to arrive at a more accurate forecast.

4. Assess the reliability of your prediction. Some events are easier to foresee than others. A meteorologist's forecast of temperatures two days from now, for example, will be more reliable than a sportscaster's prediction of the score of next year's Super Bowl. This step is intended to gauge the reliability of the forecast you made in Step 3. The goal is to estimate the correlation between the forecast and the actual outcome, expressed as a coefficient between 0 and 1, where 0 indicates no correlation and 1 indicates complete correlation. In the best case, information will be available on how well your past predictions matched the actual outcomes. You can then estimate the correlation based on historical precedent. In the absence of such information, assessments of predictability become more subjective. You may, for instance, be able to arrive at an estimate of predictability based on how the situation at hand compares with other forecasting situations. To return to the movie example, say that you are fairly confident that your ability to predict the sales of films exceeds the ability of sportscasters to predict point spreads in football games but is not as good as the ability of weather forecasters to predict temperatures two days out. Through a diligent statistical analysis, you could construct a rough scale of predictability based on computed correlations between predictions and outcomes for football scores and temperatures. You can then estimate where your ability to predict film scores lies on this scale. When the calculations are complex, it may help to bring in a skilled statistician.

(*continued*)

5. Correct the intuitive estimate. Due to bias, the intuitive estimate made in Step 3 will likely be optimistic—deviating too far from the average outcome of the reference class. In this final step, you adjust the estimate toward the average based on your analysis of predictability in Step 4. The less reliable the prediction, the more the estimate needs to be regressed toward the mean. Suppose that your intuitive prediction of a film's sales is $95 million and that, on average, films in the reference class do $40 million worth of business. Suppose further that you have estimated the correlation coefficient to be 0.6. The regressed estimate of ticket sales would be:

$$\$95M + [0.6\,(\$40M-\$95M)] = \$62M$$

As you see, the adjustment for optimism will often be substantial, particularly in highly uncertain situations where predictions are unreliable.

1. This discussion builds on "Intuitive Predictions: Biases and Corrective Procedures," a 1979 article by Daniel Kahneman and Amos Tversky that appeared in *TIMS Studies in Management Science,* volume 12 (Elsevier/North Holland).

sums of money are at stake. There needs to be a balance between optimism and realism—between goals and forecasts. Aggressive goals can motivate the troops and improve the chances of success, but outside-view forecasts should be used to decide whether or not to make a commitment in the first place.

The ideal is to draw a clear distinction between those functions and positions that involve or support decision making and those that promote or guide action. The former should be imbued with a realistic outlook, while the latter will often benefit from a sense of optimism. An optimistic CFO, for example, could mean disaster for a company, just as a lack of optimism would undermine the visionary qualities essential for superior R&D and the esprit de corps central to a successful sales force. Indeed, those charged with implementing a plan should probably not even see the outside-view forecasts, which might reduce their incentive to perform at their best.

Of course, clean distinctions between decision making and action break down at the top. CEOs, unit managers, and project champions need to be optimistic and realistic at the same time. If you happen to be in one of these positions, you should make sure that you and your planners adopt an outside view in deciding where to invest among competing initiatives. More objective forecasts will help you choose your goals wisely and your means prudently. Once an organization is committed to a course of action, however, constantly revising and reviewing the odds of success is unlikely to be good for its morale or performance. Indeed, a healthy dose of optimism will give you and your subordinates an advantage in tackling the challenges that are sure to lie ahead.

DAN LOVALLO is a senior lecturer at the Australian Graduate School of Management at the University of New South Wales. **DANIEL KAHNEMAN** is the Eugene Higgins Professor of Psychology at Princeton University.

Originally published in July 2003. Reprint R0307D

Conquering a Culture of Indecision

by Ram Charan

DOES THIS SOUND FAMILIAR? You're sitting in the quarterly business review as a colleague plows through a two-inch-thick proposal for a big investment in a new product. When he finishes, the room falls quiet. People look left, right, or down, waiting for someone else to open the discussion. No one wants to comment—at least not until the boss shows which way he's leaning.

Finally, the CEO breaks the loud silence. He asks a few mildly skeptical questions to show he's done his due diligence. But it's clear that he has made up his mind to back the project. Before long, the other meeting attendees are chiming in dutifully, careful to keep their comments positive. Judging from the remarks, it appears that everyone in the room supports the project.

But appearances can be deceiving. The head of a related division worries that the new product will take resources away from his operation. The vice president

of manufacturing thinks that the first-year sales forecasts are wildly optimistic and will leave him with a
warehouse full of unsold goods. Others in the room are
lukewarm because they don't see how they stand to
gain from the project. But they keep their reservations
to themselves, and the meeting breaks up inconclu-
sively. Over the next few months, the project is slowly
strangled to death in a series of strategy, budget, and
operational reviews. It's not clear who's responsible for
the killing, but it's plain that the true sentiment in the
room was the opposite of the apparent consensus.

In my career as an adviser to large organizations and
their leaders, I have witnessed many occasions even
at the highest levels when silent lies and a lack of
closure lead to false decisions. They are "false" because
they eventually get undone by unspoken factors and
inaction. And after a quarter century of first-hand
observations, I have concluded that these instances of
indecision share a family resemblance—a misfire in the
personal interactions that are supposed to produce
results. The people charged with reaching a decision
and acting on it fail to connect and engage with one
another. Intimidated by the group dynamics of hierarchy and constrained by formality and lack of trust, they
speak their lines woodenly and without conviction.
Lacking emotional commitment, the people who must
carry out the plan don't act decisively.

These faulty interactions rarely occur in isolation.
Far more often, they're typical of the way large and
small decisions are made—or not made—throughout a
company. The inability to take decisive action is rooted

Idea in Brief

The single greatest cause of corporate underperformance is the failure to execute. According to author Ram Charan, such failures usually result from misfires in personal interactions. And these faulty interactions rarely occur in isolation, Charan says in this article originally published in 2001. More often than not, they're typical of the way large and small decisions are made (or not made) throughout an organization. The inability to take decisive action is rooted in a company's culture. Leaders create this culture of indecisiveness, Charan says—and they can break it by doing three things: First, they must engender intellectual honesty in the connections between people. Second, they must see to it that the organization's social operating mechanisms— the meetings, reviews, and other situations through which people in the corporation transact business—have honest dialogue at their cores. And third, leaders must ensure that feedback and follow-through are used to reward high achievers, coach those who are struggling, and discourage those whose behaviors are blocking the organization's progress. By taking these three approaches and using every encounter as an opportunity to model open and honest dialogue, leaders can set the tone for an organization, moving it from paralysis to action.

in the corporate culture and seems to employees to be impervious to change.

The key word here is "seems," because, in fact, leaders create a culture of indecisiveness, and leaders can break it. The primary instrument at their disposal is the human interactions—the dialogues—through which assumptions are challenged or go unchallenged, information is shared or not shared, disagreements are brought to the surface or papered over. Dialogue is the basic unit of work in an organization. The quality of the dialogue determines how people gather and process information, how they make decisions, and how they feel about one another and about the outcome of these decisions. Dialogue can lead to new ideas and speed as a competitive advantage. It is the single-most important factor underlying the productivity and growth of the knowledge worker. Indeed, the tone and content of dialogue shapes people's behaviors and beliefs—that is, the corporate culture—faster and more permanently than any reward system, structural change, or vision statement I've seen.

Breaking a culture of indecision requires a leader who can engender intellectual honesty and trust in the connections between people. By using each encounter with his or her employees as an opportunity to model open, honest, and decisive dialogue, the leader sets the tone for the entire organization.

But setting the tone is only the first step. To transform a culture of indecision, leaders must also see to it that the organization's *social operating mechanisms*—that is, the executive committee meetings, budget and strategy reviews, and other situations through which the people of a corporation do business—have honest dialogue at their center. These mechanisms set the stage. Tightly linked and consistently practiced, they establish clear lines of accountability for reaching decisions and executing them.

Follow-through and feedback are the final steps in creating a decisive culture. Successful leaders use follow-through and honest feedback to reward high achievers, coach those who are struggling, and redirect the behaviors of those blocking the organization's progress.

In sum, leaders can create a culture of decisive behavior through attention to their own dialogue, the careful design of social operating mechanisms, and appropriate follow-through and feedback.

It All Begins with Dialogue

Studies of successful companies often focus on their products, business models, or operational strengths: Microsoft's world-conquering Windows operating system, Dell's mass customization, Wal-Mart's logistical prowess. Yet products and operational strengths aren't what really set the most successful organizations apart—they can all be rented or imitated. What can't be easily duplicated are the decisive dialogues and robust operating mechanisms and their links to feedback and follow-through. These factors constitute an organization's most enduring competitive advantage, and they are heavily dependent on the character of dialogue that a leader exhibits and thereby influences throughout the organization.

Decisive dialogue is easier to recognize than to define. It encourages incisiveness and creativity and brings coherence to seemingly fragmented and unrelated ideas. It allows tensions to surface and then resolves them by fully airing every relevant viewpoint. Because such dialogue is a process of intellectual inquiry rather than of advocacy, a search for truth rather than a contest, people feel emotionally committed to the outcome. The outcome seems "right" because people have helped shape it. They are energized and ready to act.

Not long ago, I observed the power of a leader's dialogue to shape a company's culture. The setting was the headquarters of a major U.S. multinational. The head of one of the company's largest business units was making a strategy presentation to the CEO and a few of his senior lieutenants. Sounding confident, almost cocky, the unit head laid out his strategy for taking his division from number three in Europe to number one. It was an ambitious plan that hinged on making rapid, sizable market-share gains in Germany, where the company's main competitor was locally based and four times his division's size. The CEO commended his unit head for the inspiring and visionary presentation, then initiated a dialogue to test whether the plan was realistic. "Just how are you going to make these gains?" he wondered aloud. "What other alternatives have you considered? What customers do you plan to acquire?" The unit manager hadn't thought that far ahead. "How have you defined the customers' needs in new and unique ways? How many salespeople do you have?" the CEO asked.

"Ten," answered the unit head.

"How many does your main competitor have?"

"Two hundred," came the sheepish reply.

The boss continued to press: "Who runs Germany for us? Wasn't he in another division up until about three months ago?"

Had the exchange stopped there, the CEO would have only humiliated and discouraged this unit head and sent a message to others in attendance that the risks of thinking big were unacceptably high. But the

CEO wasn't interested in killing the strategy and demoralizing the business unit team. Coaching through questioning, he wanted to inject some realism into the dialogue. Speaking bluntly, but not angrily or unkindly, he told the unit manager that he would need more than bravado to take on a formidable German competitor on its home turf. Instead of making a frontal assault, the CEO suggested, why not look for the competition's weak spots and win on speed of execution? Where are the gaps in your competitor's product line? Can you innovate something that can fill those gaps? What customers are the most likely buyers of such a product? Why not zero in on them? Instead of aiming for overall market-share gains, try resegmenting the market. Suddenly, what had appeared to be a dead end opened into new insights, and by the end of the meeting, it was decided that the manager would rethink the strategy and return in 90 days with a more realistic alternative. A key player whose strategy proposal had been flatly rejected left the room feeling energized, challenged, and more sharply focused on the task at hand.

Think about what happened here. Although it might not have been obvious at first, the CEO was not trying to assert his authority or diminish the executive. He simply wanted to ensure that the competitive realities were not glossed over and to coach those in attendance on both business acumen and organizational capability as well as on the fine art of asking the right questions. He was challenging the proposed strategy not for personal reasons but for business reasons.

Dialogue Killers

IS THE DIALOGUE IN YOUR meetings an energy drain? If it doesn't energize people and focus their work, watch for the following.

Dangling Dialogue

Symptom: Confusion prevails. The meeting ends without a clear next step. People create their own self-serving interpretations of the meeting, and no one can be held accountable later when goals aren't met.

Remedy: Give the meeting closure by ensuring that everyone knows who will do what, by when. Do it in writing if necessary, and be specific.

Information Clogs

Symptom: Failure to get all the relevant information into the open. An important fact or opinion comes to light after a decision has been reached, which reopens the decision. This pattern happens repeatedly.

Remedy: Ensure that the right people are in attendance in the first place. When missing information is discovered, disseminate it immediately. Make the expectation for openness and candor explicit by asking, "What's missing?" Use coaching and sanctions to correct information hoarding.

The dialogue affected people's attitudes and behavior in subtle and not so subtle ways: They walked away knowing that they should look for opportunities in unconventional ways and be prepared to answer the inevitable tough questions. They also knew that the CEO was on their side. They became more convinced that growth was possible and that action was necessary. And

Piecemeal Perspectives

Symptom: People stick to narrow views and self-interests and fail to acknowledge that others have valid interests.

Remedy: Draw people out until you're sure all sides of the issue have been represented. Restate the common purpose repeatedly to keep everyone focused on the big picture. Generate alternatives. Use coaching to show people how their work contributes to the overall mission of the enterprise.

Free-for-All

Symptom: By failing to direct the flow of the discussion, the leader allows negative behaviors to flourish. "Extortionists" hold the whole group for ransom until others see it their way; "sidetrackers" go off on tangents, recount history by saying "When I did this ten years ago . . .," or delve into unnecessary detail; "silent liars" do not express their true opinions, or they agree to things they have no intention of doing; and "dividers" create breaches within the group by seeking support for their viewpoint outside the social operating mechanism or have parallel discussions during the meeting.

Remedy: The leader must exercise inner strength by repeatedly signaling which behaviors are acceptable and by sanctioning those who persist in negative behavior. If less severe sanctions fail, the leader must be willing to remove the offending player from the group.

something else happened: They began to adopt the CEO's tone in subsequent meetings. When, for example, the head of the German unit met with his senior staff to brief them on the new approach to the German market, the questions he fired at his sales chief and product development head were pointed, precise, and aimed directly at putting the new strategy into action.

He had picked up on his boss's style of relating to others as well as his way of eliciting, sifting, and analyzing information. The entire unit grew more determined and energized.

The chief executive didn't leave the matter there, though. He followed up with a one-page, handwritten letter to the unit head stating the essence of the dialogue and the actions to be executed. And in 90 days, they met again to discuss the revised strategy. (For more on fostering decisive dialogue, see the sidebar "Dialogue Killers.")

How Dialogue Becomes Action

The setting in which dialogue occurs is as important as the dialogue itself. The social operating mechanisms of decisive corporate cultures feature behaviors marked by four characteristics: openness, candor, informality, and closure. Openness means that the outcome is not predetermined. There's an honest search for alternatives and new discoveries. Questions like "What are we missing?" draw people in and signal the leader's willingness to hear all sides. Leaders create an atmosphere of safety that permits spirited discussion, group learning, and trust.

Candor is slightly different. It's a willingness to speak the unspeakable, to expose unfulfilled commitments, to air the conflicts that undermine apparent consensus. Candor means that people express their real opinions, not what they think team players are supposed to say. Candor helps wipe out the silent lies and pocket vetoes that occur when people agree to things they have no intention of acting on. It prevents the kind of unnecessary rework and revisiting of decisions that saps productivity.

Formality suppresses candor; informality encourages it. When presentations and comments are stiff and prepackaged, they signal that the whole meeting has been carefully scripted and orchestrated. Informality has the opposite effect. It reduces defensiveness. People feel more comfortable asking questions and reacting honestly, and the spontaneity is energizing.

If informality loosens the atmosphere, closure imposes discipline. Closure means that at the end of the meeting, people know exactly what they are expected to do. Closure produces decisiveness by assigning accountability and deadlines to people in an open forum. It tests a leader's inner strength and intellectual resources. Lack of closure, coupled with a lack of sanctions, is the primary reason for a culture of indecision.

A robust social operating mechanism consistently includes these four characteristics. Such a mechanism has the right people participating in it, and it occurs with the right frequency.

When Dick Brown arrived at Electronic Data Systems (EDS) in early 1999, he resolved to create a culture that did more than pay lip service to the ideals of collaboration, openness, and decisiveness. He had a big job ahead of him. EDS was known for its bright, aggressive people, but employees had a reputation for competing against one another at least as often as they pulled together. The organization was marked by a culture of lone heroes. Individual operating units had little or no incentive for sharing information or cooperating with one another to win business. There were few sanctions for "lone" behaviors and for failure to meet performance goals. And indecision was rife. As one company veteran puts it, "Meetings, meetings, and more meetings. People couldn't make decisions, wouldn't make decisions. They didn't have to. No accountability." EDS was losing business. Revenue was flat, earnings were on the decline, and the price of the company's stock was down sharply.

A central tenet of Brown's management philosophy is that "leaders get the behavior they tolerate." Shortly after he arrived at EDS, he installed six social operating mechanisms within one year that signaled he would not put up with the old culture of rampant individualism and information hoarding. One mechanism was the "performance call," as it is known around the company. Once a month, the top 100 or so EDS executives worldwide take part in a conference call where the past month's numbers and critical activities are reviewed in detail. Transparency and simultaneous information are the rules; information hoarding is no longer possible. Everyone knows who is on target for the year, who is ahead of projections, and who is behind. Those who are behind must explain the shortfall—and how they plan to get back on track. It's not enough for a manager to say she's assessing, reviewing, or analyzing a problem. Those aren't the words of someone who is acting, Brown says. Those are the words of someone getting ready to act. To use them in front of Brown is to invite two questions in response: When you've finished your analysis, what are you going to do? And how soon are you going to do it? The only way that Brown's people can answer those questions satisfactorily is to make a decision and execute it.

The performance calls are also a mechanism for airing and resolving the conflicts inevitable in a large organization, particularly when it comes to cross selling in order to accelerate revenue growth. Two units may be pursuing the same customer, for example, or a customer serviced by one unit may be acquired by a customer serviced by another. Which unit should lead the pursuit? Which unit should service the merged entity? It's vitally important to resolve these questions. Letting them fester doesn't just drain emotional energy, it shrinks the organization's capacity to act decisively. Lack of speed becomes a competitive disadvantage.

Brown encourages people to bring these conflicts to the surface, both because he views them as a sign of organizational health and because they provide an opportunity to demonstrate the style of dialogue he advocates. He tries to create a safe environment for disagreement by reminding employees that the conflict isn't personal.

Conflict in any global organization is built in. And, Brown believes, it's essential if everyone is going to think in terms of the entire organization, not just one little corner of it. Instead of seeking the solution favorable to their unit, they'll look for the solution that's best for EDS and its shareholders. It sounds simple, even obvious. But in an organization once characterized by

GE's Secret Weapon

KNOWN FOR ITS STATE-OF-THE-ART management practices, General Electric has forged a system of ten tightly linked social operating mechanisms. Vital to GE's success, these mechanisms set goals and priorities for the whole company as well as for its individual business units and track each unit's progress toward those goals. CEO Jack Welch also uses the system to evaluate senior managers within each unit and reward or sanction them according to their performance.

Three of the most widely imitated of these mechanisms are the Corporate Executive Council (CEC), which meets four times a year; the annual leadership and organizational reviews, known as Session C; and the annual strategy reviews, known as S-1 and S-2. Most large organizations have similar mechanisms. GE's, however, are notable for their intensity and duration; tight links to one another; follow-through; and uninhibited candor, closure, and decisiveness.

At the CEC, the company's senior leaders gather for two-and-a-half days of intensive collaboration and information exchange. As these leaders share best practices, assess the external business environment, and identify the company's most promising opportunities and most pressing problems, Welch has a chance to coach managers and observe their styles of working, thinking, and collaborating. Among the ten initiatives to emerge from these meetings in the past 14 years are GE's Six Sigma quality-improvement drive and its companywide e-commerce effort. These sessions aren't for the fainthearted—at times, the debates can resemble verbal combat. But by the time the CEC breaks up, everyone in attendance knows both what the corporate priorities are and what's expected of him or her.

At Session C meetings, Welch and GE's senior vice president for human resources, Bill Conaty, meet with the head of each business unit as well as his or her top HR executive to discuss leadership and organizational issues. In these intense 12- to 14-hour sessions, the attendees review the unit's prospective talent pool and its organizational priorities. Who needs to be promoted, rewarded, and developed? How? Who isn't making the grade? Candor is mandatory, and so is execution. The dialogue goes back and forth and links with the strategy of the business unit. Welch follows up each session with a handwritten note reviewing the substance of the dialogue and action items. Through this mechanism, picking and evaluating people has become a core competence at GE. No wonder GE is known as "CEO University."

The unit head's progress in implementing that action plan is among the items on the agenda at the S-1 meeting, held about two months after Session C. Welch, his chief financial officer, and members of the office of the CEO meet individually with each unit head and his or her team to discuss strategy for the next three years. The strategy, which must incorporate the companywide themes and initiatives that emerged from the CEC meetings, is subjected to intensive scrutiny and reality testing by Welch and the senior staff. The dialogue in the sessions is informal, open, decisive, and full of valuable coaching from Welch on both business and human resources issues. As in Session C, the dialogue about strategy links with people and organizational issues. Again, Welch follows up with a handwritten note in which he sets out what he expects of the unit head as a result of the dialogue.

S-2 meetings, normally held in November, follow a similar agenda to the S-1 meeting, except that they are focused on a shorter time horizon, usually 12 to 15 months. Here, operational priorities and resource allocations are linked.

Taken together, the meetings link feedback, decision making, and assessment of the organization's capabilities and key people. The mechanism explicitly ties the goals and performance of each unit to the overall strategy of the corporation and places a premium on the development of the next generation of leaders. The process is unrelenting in its demand for managerial accountability. At the same time, Welch takes the opportunity to engage in follow-through and feedback that is candid, on point, and focused on decisiveness and execution. This operating system may be GE's most enduring competitive advantage.

lone heroes and self-interest, highly visible exercises in conflict resolution remind people to align their interests with the company as a whole. It's not enough to state the message once and assume it will sink in. Behavior is changed through repetition. Stressing the message over and over in social operating mechanisms like the monthly performance calls—and rewarding or sanctioning people based on their adherence to it—is one of Brown's most powerful tools for producing the behavioral changes that usher in genuine cultural change.

Of course, no leader can or should attend every meeting, resolve every conflict, or make every decision. But by designing social operating mechanisms that promote free-flowing yet productive dialogue, leaders strongly influence how others perform these tasks. Indeed, it is through these mechanisms that the work of shaping a decisive culture gets done.

Another corporation that employs social operating mechanisms to create a decisive culture is multinational pharmaceutical giant Pharmacia. The company's approach illustrates a point I stress repeatedly to my clients: Structure divides; social operating mechanisms integrate. I hasten to add that structure is essential. If an organization didn't divide tasks, functions, and responsibilities, it would never get anything done. But social operating mechanisms are required to direct the various activities contained within a structure toward an objective. Well-designed mechanisms perform this integrating function. But no matter how well designed, the mechanisms also need decisive dialogue to work properly.

Two years after its 1995 merger with Upjohn, Pharmacia's CEO Fred Hassan set out to create an entirely new culture for the combined entity. The organization he envisioned would be collaborative, customer focused, and speedy. It would meld the disparate talents of a global enterprise to develop market-leading drugs—and do so faster than the competition. The primary mechanism for fostering collaboration: Leaders from several units and functions would engage in frequent, constructive dialogue.

The company's race to develop a new generation of antibiotics to treat drug-resistant infections afforded Pharmacia's management an opportunity to test the success of its culture-building efforts. Dr. Göran Ando, the chief of research and development, and Carrie Cox, the head of global business management, jointly created a social operating mechanism comprising some of the company's leading scientists, clinicians, and marketers. Just getting the three functions together regularly was a bold step. Typically, drug development proceeds by a series of handoffs. One group of scientists does the basic work of drug discovery, then hands off its results to a second group, which steers the drug through a year or more of clinical trials. If and when it receives the Food and Drug Administration's stamp of approval, it's handed off to the marketing people, who devise a marketing plan. Only then is the drug handed off to the sales department, which pitches it to doctors and hospitals. By supplanting this daisy-chain approach with one that made scientists, clinicians, and marketers jointly responsible for the entire flow of development and marketing, the two leaders aimed to develop a drug that better met the needs of patients, had higher revenue potential, and gained speed as a competitive advantage. And they wanted to create a template for future collaborative efforts.

The company's reward system reinforced this collaborative model by explicitly linking compensation to the actions of the group. Every member's compensation would be based on the time to bring the drug to market, the time for the drug to reach peak profitable share, and total sales. The system gave group members a strong incentive to talk openly with one another and to share information freely. But the creative spark was missing. The first few times the drug development group met, it focused almost exclusively on their differences, which were considerable. Without trafficking in clichés, it is safe to say that scientists, clinicians, and marketers tend to have different ways of speaking, thinking, and relating. And each tended to defend what it viewed as its interests rather than the interests of shareholders and customers. It was at this point that Ando and Cox took charge of the dialogue, reminding the group that it was important to play well with others but even more important to produce a drug that met patients' needs and to beat the competition.

Acting together, the two leaders channeled conversation into productive dialogue focused on a common task. They shared what they knew about developing and marketing pharmaceuticals and demonstrated how scientists could learn to think a little like marketers, and marketers a little like scientists. They tackled the emotional challenge of resolving conflicts in the open in order to demonstrate how to disagree, sometimes strongly, without animosity and without losing sight of their common purpose.

Indeed, consider how one dialogue helped the group make a decision that turned a promising drug into a success story. To simplify the research and testing process, the group's scientists had begun to search for an antibiotic that would be effective against a limited number of infections and would be used only as "salvage therapy" in acute cases, when conventional antibiotic therapies had failed. But intensive dialogue with the marketers yielded the information that doctors were receptive to a drug that would work against a wide spectrum of infections. They wanted a drug that could treat acute infections completely by starting treatment earlier in the course of the disease, either in large doses through an intravenous drip or in smaller doses with a pill. The scientists shifted their focus, and the result was Zyvox, one of the major pharmaceutical success stories of recent years. It has become the poster drug in Pharmacia's campaign for a culture characterized by cross-functional collaboration and speedy execution. Through dialogue, the group created a product that neither the scientists, clinicians, nor marketers acting by themselves could have envisioned or executed. And the mechanism that created this open dialogue is now standard practice at Pharmacia.

Follow-Through and Feedback

Follow-through is in the DNA of decisive cultures and takes place either in person, on the telephone, or in the routine conduct of a social operating mechanism. Lack of follow-through destroys the discipline of execution and encourages indecision.

A culture of indecision changes when groups of people are compelled to always be direct. And few mechanisms encourage directness more effectively than performance and compensation reviews, especially if they are explicitly linked to social operating mechanisms. Yet all too often, the performance review process is as ritualized and empty as the business meeting I described at the beginning of this article. Both the employee and his manager want to get the thing over with as quickly as possible. Check the appropriate box, keep up the good work, here's your raise, and let's be sure to do this again next year. Sorry—gotta run. There's no genuine conversation, no feedback, and worst of all, no chance for the employee to learn the sometimes painful truths that will help her grow and develop. Great compensation systems die for lack of candid dialogue and leaders' emotional fortitude.

At EDS, Dick Brown has devised an evaluation and review process that virtually forces managers to engage in candid dialogue with their subordinates. Everyone at the company is ranked in quintiles and rewarded according to how well they perform compared with their peers. It has proved to be one of the most controversial features of Dick Brown's leadership—some employees view it as a Darwinian means of dividing winners from losers and pitting colleagues against one another.

That isn't the objective of the ranking system, Brown insists. He views the ranking process as the most effective way to reward the company's best performers and show laggards where they need to improve. But the system needs the right sort of dialogue to make it work as intended and serve its purpose of growing the talent pool. Leaders must give honest feedback to their direct reports, especially to those who find themselves at the bottom of the rankings.

Brown recalls one encounter he had shortly after the first set of rankings was issued. An employee who had considered himself one of EDS's best performers was shocked to find himself closer to the bottom of the roster than the top. "How could this be?" the employee asked. "I performed as well this year as I did last year, and last year my boss gave me a stellar review." Brown replied that he could think of two possible explanations. The first was that the employee wasn't as good at his job as he thought he was. The second possibility was that even if the employee was doing as good a job as he did the previous year, his peers were doing better. "If you're staying the same," Brown concluded, "you're falling behind."

That exchange revealed the possibility—the likelihood, even—that the employee's immediate superior had given him a less-than-honest review the year before rather than tackle the unpleasant task of telling him where he was coming up short. Brown understands why a manager might be tempted to duck such a painful conversation. Delivering negative feedback tests the strength of a leader. But critical feedback is part of what Brown calls "the heavy lifting of leadership." Avoiding it, he says, "sentences the organization to mediocrity."

What's more, by failing to provide honest feedback, leaders cheat their people by depriving them of the information they need to improve.

Feedback should be many things—candid; constructive; relentlessly focused on behavioral performance, accountability, and execution. One thing it shouldn't be is surprising. "A leader should be constructing his appraisal all year long," Brown says, "and giving his appraisal all year long. You have 20, 30, 60 opportunities a year to share your observations. Don't let those opportunities pass. If, at the end of the year, someone is truly surprised by what you have to say, that's a failure of leadership."

Ultimately, changing a culture of indecision is a matter of leadership. It's a matter of asking hard questions: How robust and effective are our social operating mechanisms? How well are they linked? Do they have the right people and the right frequency? Do they have a rhythm and operate consistently? Is follow-through built in? Are rewards and sanctions linked to the outcomes of the decisive dialogue? Most important, how productive is the dialogue within these mechanisms? Is our dialogue marked by openness, candor, informality, and closure?

Transforming a culture of indecision is an enormous and demanding task. It takes all the listening skills, business acumen, and operational experience that a corporate leader can summon. But just as important, the job demands emotional fortitude, follow-through, and inner strength. Asking the right questions; identifying and resolving conflicts; providing candid, constructive feedback; and differentiating people with sanctions and rewards is never easy. Frequently, it's downright unpleasant. No wonder many senior executives avoid the task. In the short term, they spare themselves considerable emotional wear and tear. But their evasion sets the tone for an organization that can't share intelligence, make decisions, or face conflicts, much less resolve them. Those who evade miss the very point of effective leadership. Leaders with the strength to insist on honest dialogue and follow-through will be rewarded not only with a decisive organization but also with a workforce that is energized, empowered, and engaged.

RAM CHARAN is a former faculty member of Harvard Business School and Northwestern University's Kellogg School of Management.

Originally published in April 2001. Reprint R0601J

Evidence-Based Management

by Jeffrey Pfeffer and Robert I. Sutton

A BOLD NEW WAY OF thinking has taken the medical establishment by storm in the past decade: the idea that decisions in medical care should be based on the latest and best knowledge of what actually works. Dr. David Sackett, the individual most associated with *evidence-based medicine,* defines it as "the conscientious, explicit and judicious use of current best evidence in making decisions about the care of individual patients." Sackett, his colleagues at McMaster University in Ontario, Canada, and the growing number of physicians joining the movement are committed to identifying, disseminating, and, most importantly, applying research that is soundly conducted and clinically relevant.

If all this sounds laughable to you—after all, what else besides evidence *would* guide medical decisions?— then you are woefully naive about how doctors have traditionally plied their trade. Yes, the research is out there—thousands of studies are conducted on medical practices and products every year. Unfortunately, physicians don't use much of it. Recent studies show that only about 15% of their decisions are evidence based. For the most part, here's what doctors rely on instead: obsolete knowledge gained in school, long-standing but never proven traditions, patterns gleaned from experience, the methods they believe in and are most skilled in applying, and information from hordes of vendors with products and services to sell.

The same behavior holds true for managers looking to cure their organizational ills. Indeed, we would argue, managers are actually much more ignorant than doctors about which prescriptions are reliable—and they're less eager to find out. If doctors practiced medicine like many companies practice management, there would be more unnecessarily sick or dead patients and many more doctors in jail or suffering other penalties for malpractice.

It's time to start an evidence-based movement in the ranks of managers. Admittedly, in some ways, the challenge is greater here than in medicine. (See the sidebar "What Makes It Hard to Be Evidence Based?") The evidence is weaker; almost anyone can (and often does) claim to be a management expert; and a bewildering array of sources—Shakespeare, Billy Graham, Jack Welch, Tony Soprano, fighter pilots, Santa Claus, Attila the Hun—are used to generate management advice. Managers seeking the best evidence also face a more vexing problem than physicians do: Because companies vary so wildly in size, form, and age, compared with human beings, it is far more risky in business to presume that a proven "cure" developed in one place will be effective elsewhere.

Idea in Brief

For the most part, managers looking to cure their organizational ills rely on obsolete knowledge they picked up in school, long-standing but never proven traditions, patterns gleaned from experience, methods they happen to be skilled in applying, and information from vendors. They could learn a thing or two from practitioners of evidence-based medicine, a movement that has taken the medical establishment by storm over the past decade. A growing number of physicians are eschewing the usual, flawed resources and are instead identifying, disseminating, and applying research that is soundly conducted and clinically relevant. It's time for managers to do the same. The challenge is, quite simply, to ground decisions in the latest and best knowledge of what actually works. In some ways, that's more difficult to do in business than in medicine. The evidence is weaker in business; almost anyone can (and many people do) claim to be a management expert; and a motley crew of sources—Shakespeare, Billy Graham, Jack Welch, Attila the Hun—are used to generate management advice. Still, it makes sense that when managers act on better logic and strong evidence, their companies will beat the competition. Like medicine, management is learned through practice and experience. Yet managers (like doctors) can practice their craft more effectively if they relentlessly seek new knowledge and insight, from both inside and outside their companies, so they can keep updating their assumptions, skills, and knowledge.

Still, it makes sense that when managers act on better logic and evidence, their companies will trump the competition. That is why we've spent our entire research careers, especially the last five years, working to develop and surface the best evidence on how companies ought to be managed and teaching managers the right mind-set and methods for practicing evidence-based management. As with medicine, management is and will likely always be a craft that can be learned only

What Makes It Hard to Be Evidence Based?

YOU MAY WELL BE TRYING to bring the best evidence to bear on your decisions. You follow the business press, buy business books, hire consultants, and attend seminars featuring business experts. But evidence-based management is still hard to apply. Here's what you're up against.

There's Too Much Evidence

With hundreds of English-language magazines and journals devoted to business and management issues, dozens of business newspapers, roughly 30,000 business books in print and thousands more being published each year, and the Web-based outlets for business knowledge continuing to expand (ranging from online versions of *Fortune* and the *Wall Street Journal* to specialized sites like Hr.com and Gantthead.com), it is fair to say that there is simply too much information for any manager to consume. Moreover, recommendations about management practice are seldom integrated in a way that makes them accessible or memorable. Consider, for instance, *Business: The Ultimate Resource,* a tome that weighs about eight pounds and runs 2,208 oversize pages. *Business* claims that it "will become the 'operating system' for any organization or anyone in business." But a good operating system fits together in a seamless and logical manner—not the case here or with any such encyclopedic effort to date.

There's Not Enough Good Evidence

Despite the existence of "data, data everywhere," managers still find themselves parched for reliable guidance. In 1993, senior Bain consultant Darrell Rigby began conducting the only survey we have encountered on the use and persistence of various management tools and techniques. (Findings from the most recent version of Bain's Management Tools survey were published in *Strategy and Leadership* in 2005.) Rigby told us it struck him as odd that you could get good information on products such as toothpaste and cereal but almost no information about interventions that companies were spending millions of dollars to implement. Even the Bain survey, noteworthy as it is, measures only the degree to which the different programs are used and does not go beyond subjective assessments of their value.

The Evidence Doesn't Quite Apply

Often, managers are confronted with half-truths—advice that is true some of the time, under certain conditions. Take, for example, the controversy around stock options. The evidence suggests that, in general, heavier reliance on stock options does not increase a firm's performance, but it does increase the chances that a company will need to restate its earnings. However, in small, privately held start-ups, options do appear to be relevant to success and less likely to produce false hype. One hallmark of solid research is conservatism—the carefulness of the researcher to point out the specific context in which intervention A led to outcome B. Unfortunately, that leaves managers wondering if the research could possibly be relevant to them.

People Are Trying to Mislead You

Because it's so hard to distinguish good advice from bad, managers are constantly enticed to believe in and implement flawed business practices. A big part of the problem is consultants, who are *always* rewarded for getting work, only *sometimes* rewarded for doing good work, and *hardly ever* rewarded for evaluating whether they have actually improved things. Worst of all, if a client's problems are only partly solved, that leads to more work for the consulting firm! (If you think our charge is too harsh, ask the people at your favorite consulting firm what evidence they have that their advice or techniques actually work—and pay attention to the evidence they offer.)

You Are Trying to Mislead You

Simon and Garfunkel were right when they sang, "A man hears what he wants to hear and disregards the rest." Many practitioners

(continued)

and their advisers routinely ignore evidence about management practices that clashes with their beliefs and ideologies, and their own observations are contaminated by what they expect to see. This is especially dangerous because some theories can become self-fulfilling—that is, we sometimes perpetuate our pet theories with our own actions. If we expect people to be untrustworthy, for example, we will closely monitor their behavior, which makes it impossible to develop trust. (Meanwhile, experimental evidence shows that when people are placed in situations where authority figures expect them to cheat, more of them do, in fact, cheat.)

The Side Effects Outweigh the Cure

Sometimes, evidence points clearly to a cure, but the effects of the cure are too narrowly considered. One of our favorite examples comes from outside management, in the controversy over social promotion in public schools—that is, advancing a child to the next grade even if his or her work isn't up to par. Former U.S. president Bill Clinton represented the views of many when, in his 1999 State of the Union address, he said, "We do our children no favors when we allow them to pass from grade to grade without mastering the material." President George W. Bush holds the same view. But this belief is contrary to the results from over 55 published studies that demonstrate the net negative effects of ending social promotion (versus no careful studies that find positive effects). Many school systems that have tried to end the practice have quickly discovered the fly in the ointment: Holding students back leaves schools

through practice and experience. Yet we believe that managers (like doctors) can practice their craft more effectively if they are routinely guided by the best logic and evidence—and if they relentlessly seek new knowledge and insight, from both inside and outside crowded with older students, and costs skyrocket as more teachers and other resources are needed because the average student spends more years in school. The flunked kids also consistently come out worse in the end, with lower test scores and higher dropout rates. There are also reports that bullying increases: Those flunked kids, bigger than their classmates, are mad about being held back, and the teachers have trouble maintaining control in the larger classes.

Stories Are More Persuasive, Anyway

It's hard to remain devoted to the task of building bulletproof, evidence-based cases for action when it's clear that good storytelling often carries the day. And indeed, we reject the notion that only quantitative data should qualify as evidence. As Einstein put it, "Not everything that can be counted counts, and not everything that counts can be counted." When used correctly, stories and cases are powerful tools for building management knowledge. Many quantitative studies are published on developing new products, but few come close to Tracy Kidder's Pulitzer-winning *Soul of a New Machine* in capturing how engineers develop products and how managers can enhance or undermine the engineers' (and products') success. Gordon MacKenzie's *Orbiting the Giant Hairball* is the most charming and useful book on corporate creativity we know. Good stories have their place in an evidence-based world, in suggesting hypotheses, augmenting other (often quantitative) research, and rallying people who will be affected by a change.

their companies, to keep updating their assumptions, knowledge, and skills. We aren't there yet, but we are getting closer. The managers and companies that come closest already enjoy a pronounced competitive advantage.

What Passes for Wisdom

If a doctor or a manager makes a decision that is not based on the current best evidence of what may work, then what is to blame? It may be tempting to think the worst. Stupidity. Laziness. Downright deceit. But the real answer is more benign. Seasoned practitioners sometimes neglect to seek out new evidence because they trust their own clinical experience more than they trust research. Most of them would admit problems with the small sample size that characterizes personal observation, but nonetheless, information acquired firsthand often feels richer and closer to real knowledge than do words and data in a journal article. Lots of managers, likewise, get their companies into trouble by importing, without sufficient thought, performance management and measurement practices from their past experience. We saw this at a small software company, where the chair of the compensation committee, a successful and smart executive, recommended the compensation policies he had employed at his last firm. The fact that the two companies were dramatically different in size, sold different kinds of software, used different distribution methods, and targeted different markets and customers didn't seem to faze him or many of his fellow committee members.

Another alternative to using evidence is making decisions that capitalize on the practitioner's own strengths. This is particularly a problem with specialists, who default to the treatments with which they have the most experience and skill. Surgeons are notorious for it. (One doctor and author, Melvin Konner, cites a common joke amongst his peers: "If you want to have an operation, ask a surgeon if you need one.") Similarly, if your business needs to drum up leads, your event planner is likely to recommend an event, and your direct marketers will probably suggest a mailing. The old saying "To a hammer, everything looks like a nail" often explains what gets done.

Hype and marketing, of course, also play a role in what information reaches the busy practitioner. Doctors face an endless supply of vendors, who muddy the waters by exaggerating the benefits and downplaying the risks of using their drugs and other products. Meanwhile, some truly efficacious solutions have no particularly interested advocates behind them. For years, general physicians have referred patients with plantar warts on their feet to specialists for expensive and painful surgical procedures. Only recently has word got out that duct tape does the trick just as well.

Numerous other decisions are driven by dogma and belief. When people are overly influenced by ideology, they often fail to question whether a practice will work—it fits so well with what they "know" about what makes people and organizations tick. In business, the use and defense of stock options as a compensation strategy seems to be just such a case of cherished belief trumping evidence, to the detriment of organizations. Many executives maintain that options produce an ownership culture that encourages 80-hour workweeks, frugality with the company's money, and a host of personal sacrifices in the interest of value creation.

T.J. Rodgers, chief executive of Cypress Semiconductor, typifies this mind-set. He told the *San Francisco Chronicle* that without options, "I would no longer have employee shareholders, I would just have employees." There is, in fact, little evidence that equity incentives of any kind, including stock options, enhance organizational performance. A recent review of more than 220 studies compiled by Indiana University's Dan R. Dalton and colleagues concluded that equity ownership had no consistent effects on financial performance.

Ideology is also to blame for the persistence of the first-mover-advantage myth. Research by Wharton's Lisa Bolton demonstrates that most people—whether experienced in business or naive about it—believe that the first company to enter an industry or market will have a big advantage over competitors. Yet empirical evidence is actually quite mixed as to whether such an advantage exists, and many "success stories" purported to support the first-mover advantage turn out to be false. (Amazon.com, for instance, was not the first company to start selling books online.) In Western culture, people believe that the early bird gets the worm, yet this is a half-truth. As futurist Paul Saffo puts it, the whole truth is that the second (or third or fourth) mouse often gets the cheese. Unfortunately, beliefs in the power of being first and fastest in everything we do are so ingrained that giving people contradictory evidence does not cause them to abandon their faith in the first-mover advantage. Beliefs rooted in ideology or in cultural values are quite "sticky," resist disconfirmation, and persist in affecting judgments and choice, regardless of whether they are true.

Finally, there is the problem of uncritical emulation and its business equivalent: casual benchmarking. Both doctors and managers look to perceived high performers in their field and try to mimic those top dogs' moves. We aren't damning benchmarking in general—it can be a powerful and cost-efficient tool. (See the sidebar "Can Benchmarking Produce Evidence?") Yet it is important to remember that if you only copy what other people or companies do, the best you can be is a perfect imitation. So the most you can hope to have are practices as good as, but no better than, those of top performers—and by the time you mimic them, they've moved on. This isn't necessarily a bad thing, as you can save time and money by learning from the experience of others inside and outside your industry. And if you consistently implement best practices better than your rivals, you will beat the competition.

Benchmarking is most hazardous to organizational health, however, when used in its "casual" form, in which the logic behind what works for top performers, why it works, and what will work elsewhere is barely unraveled. Consider a quick example. When United Airlines decided in 1994 to try to compete with Southwest in the California market, it tried to imitate Southwest. United created a new service, Shuttle by United, with separate crews and planes (all of them Boeing 737s). The gate staff and flight attendants wore casual clothes. Passengers weren't served food. Seeking to emulate Southwest's legendary quick turnarounds and enhanced productivity, Shuttle by United increased the frequency of its flights and reduced the scheduled time

Can Benchmarking Produce Evidence?

ACROSS THE BOARD, U.S. AUTOMOBILE companies have for decades benchmarked Toyota, the world leader in auto manufacturing. In particular, many have tried to copy its factory-floor practices. They've installed just-in-time inventory systems, statistical process control charts, and pull cords to stop the assembly line if defects are noticed. Yet, although they (most notably, General Motors) have made progress, for the most part the companies still lag behind Toyota in productivity—the hours required to assemble a car—and often in quality and design as well.

Studies of the automobile industry, especially those by Wharton professor John Paul MacDuffie, suggest that the U.S. companies fell prey to the same pair of fundamental problems we have seen in so many casual-benchmarking initiatives. First, people mimic the most visible, the most obvious, and, frequently, the least important practices. The secret to Toyota's success is not a set of techniques per se, but the philosophy of total quality management and continuous improvement the company has embraced, as well as managers' accessibility to employees on the plant floor, which enables Toyota to tap these workers' tacit knowledge. Second, companies have different strategies, cultures, workforces, and competitive environments—so that what one of them needs to do to be successful is different from what others need to do. The Toyota system presumes that people will be team players and subordinate their egos for the good of the group, a collectivistic mind-set that tends to fit Asian managers and workers better than it does U.S. and European managers and workers.

Before you run off to benchmark, possibly spending effort and money that will result in no payoff or, worse yet, problems that you never had before, ask yourself the following questions:

- *Do sound logic and evidence indicate that the benchmarking target's success is attributable to the practice we seek to emulate?* Southwest Airlines is the most successful airline in the history of the industry. Herb Kelleher, its CEO from 1982 to

2001, drinks a lot of Wild Turkey bourbon. Does this mean that your company will dominate its industry if your CEO drinks a lot of Wild Turkey?

- *Are the conditions at our company—strategy, business model, workforce—similar enough to those at the benchmarked company to make the learning useful?* Just as doctors who do neurosurgery learn mostly from other neurosurgeons, not from orthopedists, you and your company should seek to learn from *relevant* others.

- *Why does a given practice enhance performance? And what is the logic that links it to bottom-line results?* If you can't explain the underlying theory, you are likely engaging in superstitious learning, and you may be copying something irrelevant or even damaging—or only copying part (perhaps the worst part) of the practice. As senior GE executives once pointed out to us, many companies that imitate their "rank and yank" system take only the A, B, and C rankings and miss the crucial subtlety that an A player is someone who helps colleagues do their jobs more effectively, rather than engaging in dysfunctional internal competition.

- *What are the downsides of implementing the practice even if it is a good idea overall?* Keep in mind that there is usually at least one disadvantage. For example, research by Mary Benner at Wharton and Michael Tushman at Harvard Business School shows that firms in the paint and photography industries that implemented more extensive process management programs did increase short-term efficiency but had more trouble keeping up with rapid technological changes. You need to ask if there are ways of mitigating the downsides, maybe even solutions that your benchmarking target uses that you aren't seeing. Say you are doing a merger. Look closely at what Cisco does and why, as it consistently profits from mergers while most other firms consistently fail.

planes would be on the ground. None of this, however, reproduced the essence of Southwest's advantage—the company's culture and management philosophy, and the priority placed on employees. Southwest wound up with an even higher market share in California after United had launched its new service. The Shuttle is now shuttered.

We've just suggested no less than six substitutes that managers, like doctors, often use for the best evidence—obsolete knowledge, personal experience, specialist skills, hype, dogma, and mindless mimicry of top performers—so perhaps it's apparent why evidence-based decision making is so rare. At the same time, it should be clear that relying on any of these six is not the best way to think about or decide among alternative practices. We'll soon describe how evidence-based management takes shape in the companies we've seen practice it. First, though, it is useful to get an example on the table of the type of issue that companies can address with better evidence.

An Example: Should We Adopt Forced Ranking?

The decision-making process used at Oxford's Centre for Evidence-Based Medicine starts with a crucial first step—the situation confronting the practitioner must be framed as an answerable question. That makes it clear how to compile relevant evidence. And so we do that here, raising a question that many companies have faced in recent years: Should we adopt forced ranking of our employees? The question refers to what General Electric more formally calls a forced-curve performance-ranking system. It's a talent management approach in which the performance levels of individuals are plotted along a bell curve. Depending on their position on the curve, employees fall into groups, with perhaps the top 20%, the so-called A players, being given outsize rewards; the middle 70% or so, the B players, being targeted for development; and the lowly bottom 10%, the C players, being counseled or thrown out of their jobs.

Without a doubt, this question arose for many companies as they engaged in benchmarking. General Electric has enjoyed great financial success and seems well stocked with star employees. GE alums have gone on to serve as CEOs at many other companies, including 3M, Boeing, Intuit, Honeywell, and the Home Depot. Systems that give the bulk of rewards to star employees have also been thoroughly hyped in business publications—for instance, in the McKinsey-authored book *The War for Talent*. But it's far from clear that the practice is worth emulating. It isn't just the infamous Enron—much praised in *The War for Talent*—that makes us say this. A couple of years ago, one of us gave a speech at a renowned but declining high-technology firm that used forced ranking (there, it was called a "stacking system"). A senior executive told us about an anonymous poll conducted among the firm's top 100 or so executives to discover which company practices made it difficult to turn knowledge into action. The stacking system was voted the worst culprit.

Would evidence-based management have kept that company from adopting this deeply unpopular program?

We think so. First, managers would have immediately questioned whether their company was similar enough to GE in various respects that a practice cribbed from it could be expected to play out in the same way. Then, they would have been compelled to take a harder look at the data presumably supporting forced ranking—the claim that this style of talent management actually has caused adherents to be more successful. So, for example, they might have noticed a key flaw in *The War for Talent*'s research method: The authors report in the appendix that companies were first rated as high or average performers, based on return to shareholders during the prior three to ten years; then interviews and surveys were conducted to measure how these firms were fighting the talent wars. So, for the 77 companies (of 141 studied), management practices assessed in 1997 were treated as the "cause" of firm performance between 1987 and 1997. The study therefore violates a fundamental condition of causality: The proposed cause needs to occur *before* the proposed effect.

Next, management would have assembled more evidence and weighed the negative against the positive. In doing so, it would have found plenty of evidence that performance improves with team continuity and time in position—two reasons to avoid the churn of what's been called the "rank and yank" approach. Think of the U.S. Women's National Soccer Team, which has won numerous championships, including two of the four Women's World Cups and two of the three Olympic women's tournaments held to date. The team certainly has had enormously talented players, such as Mia Hamm, Brandi

Chastain, Julie Foudy, Kristine Lilly, and Joy Fawcett. Yet all these players will tell you that the most important factor in their success was the communication, mutual understanding and respect, and ability to work together that developed during the 13 or so years that the stable core group played together. The power of such joint experience has been established in every setting examined, from string quartets to surgical teams, to top management teams, to airplane cockpit crews.

If managers at the technology firm had reviewed the best evidence, they would have also found that in work that requires cooperation (as nearly all the work in their company did), performance suffers when there is a big spread between the worst- and best-paid people—even though giving the lion's share of rewards to top performers is a hallmark of forced-ranking systems. In a Haas School of Business study of 102 business units, Douglas Cowherd and David Levine found that the greater the gap between top management's pay and that of other employees, the lower the product quality. Similar negative effects of dispersed pay have been found in longitudinal studies of top management teams, universities, and a sample of nearly 500 public companies. And in a recent Novations Group survey of more than 200 human resource professionals from companies with more than 2,500 employees, even though over half of the companies used forced ranking, the respondents reported that this approach resulted in lower productivity, inequity, skepticism, decreased employee engagement, reduced collaboration, damage to morale, and mistrust in leadership. We can find plenty of consultants and gurus who praise the power of dispersed pay, but we can't find a careful study that supports its value in settings where cooperation, co-ordination, and information sharing are crucial to performance.

Negative effects of highly dispersed pay are even seen in professional sports. Studies of baseball teams are especially interesting because, of all major professional sports, baseball calls for the least coordination among team members. But baseball still requires some cooperation—for example, between pitchers and catchers, and among infielders. And although individuals hit the ball, teammates can help one another improve their skills and break out of slumps. Notre Dame's Matt Bloom did a careful study of over 1,500 professional baseball players from 29 teams, spanning an eight-year period, which showed that players on teams with greater dispersion in pay had lower winning percentages, gate receipts, and media income.

Finally, an evidence-based approach would have surfaced data suggesting that average players can be extremely productive and that A players can founder, depending on the system they work in. Over 15 years of research in the auto industry provides compelling evidence for the power of systems over individual talent. Wharton's John Paul MacDuffie has combined quantitative studies of every automobile plant in the world with in-depth case studies to understand why some plants are more effective than others. MacDuffie has found that lean or flexible production systems—with their emphasis on teams, training, and job rotation, and their

de-emphasis on status differences among employees—
build higher-quality cars at a lower cost.

Becoming a Company of Evidence-Based Managers

It is one thing to believe that organizations would perform better if leaders knew and applied the best evidence. It is another thing to put that belief into practice.
We appreciate how hard it is for working managers and
executives to do their jobs. The demands for decisions
are relentless, information is incomplete, and even the
very best executives make many mistakes and undergo
constant criticism and second-guessing from people inside and outside their companies. In that respect, managers are like physicians who face one decision after
another: They can't possibly make the right choice
every time. Hippocrates, the famous Greek who wrote
the physicians' oath, described this plight well: "Life is
short, the art long, opportunity fleeting, experiment
treacherous, judgment difficult."

Teaching hospitals that embrace evidence-based
medicine try to overcome impediments to using it by
providing training, technologies, and work practices so
staff can take the critical results of the best studies to the
bedside. The equivalent should be done in management
settings. But it's also crucial to appreciate that evidence-
based management, like evidence-based medicine, entails a distinct mind-set that clashes with the way many
managers and companies operate. It features a willingness to put aside belief and conventional wisdom—the

dangerous half-truths that many embrace—and replace these with an unrelenting commitment to gather the necessary facts to make more informed and intelligent decisions.

As a leader in your organization, you can begin to nurture an evidence-based approach immediately by doing a few simple things that reflect the proper mindset. If you ask for evidence of efficacy every time a change is proposed, people will sit up and take notice. If you take the time to parse the logic behind that evidence, people will become more disciplined in their own thinking. If you treat the organization like an unfinished prototype and encourage trial programs, pilot studies, and experimentation—and reward learning from these activities, even when something new fails— your organization will begin to develop its own evidence base. And if you keep learning while acting on the best knowledge you have and expect your people to do the same—if you have what has been called "the attitude of wisdom"—then your company can profit from evidence-based management as you benefit from "enlightened trial and error" and the learning that occurs as a consequence.

Demand Evidence

When it comes to setting the tone for evidence-based management, we have met few chief executives on a par with Kent Thiry, the CEO of DaVita, a $2 billion operator of kidney dialysis centers headquartered in El Segundo, California. Thiry joined DaVita in October 1999, when the company was in default on its bank loans, could barely meet payroll, and was close to bankruptcy. A big part of his turnaround effort has been to educate the many facility administrators, a large proportion of them nurses, in the use of data to guide their decisions.

To ensure that the company has the information necessary to assess its operations, the senior management team and DaVita's chief technical officer, Harlan Cleaver, have been relentless in building and installing systems that help leaders at all levels understand how well they are doing. One of Thiry's mottoes is "No brag, just facts." When he stands up at DaVita Academy, a meeting of about 400 frontline employees from throughout the organization, and states that the company has the best quality of treatment in the industry, that assertion is demonstrated with specific, quantitative comparisons.

A large part of the company's culture is commitment to the quality of patient care. To reinforce this value, managers always begin reports and meetings with data on the effectiveness of the dialysis treatments and on patient health and well-being. And each facility administrator gets an eight-page report every month that shows a number of measures of the quality of care, which are summarized in a DaVita Quality Index. This emphasis on evidence also extends to management issues—administrators get information on operations, including treatments per day, teammate (employee) retention, the retention of higher-paying private pay patients, and a number of resource utilization measures such as labor hours per treatment and controllable expenses.

The most interesting thing about these monthly reports is what *isn't yet* included. DaVita COO Joe Mello explained that if a particular metric is deemed important, but the company currently lacks the ability to collect the relevant measurements, that metric is included on reports anyway, with the notation "not available." He said that the persistent mention of important measures that are missing helps motivate the company to figure out ways of gathering that information.

Many impressive aspects of DaVita's operations have contributed to the company's success, as evidenced by the 50% decrease in voluntary turnover, best-in-industry quality of patient care, and exceptional financial results. But the emphasis on evidence-based decision making in a culture that reinforces speaking the truth about how things are going is certainly another crucial component.

Examine Logic

Simply asking for backup research on proposals is insufficient to foster a true organizational commitment to evidence-based management, especially given the problems that bedevil much so-called business research. As managers or consultants make their case, pay close attention to gaps in exposition, logic, and inference. (See the sidebar "Are You Part of the Problem?") This is particularly important because, in management research, studies that use surveys or data from company records to correlate practices with various performance outcomes are far more common than experiments. Such "nonexperimental" research is useful, but care must be taken to examine the logic of the research design and to control statistically for alternative explanations, which arise in even the best studies. Managers who consume such knowledge need to understand the limitations and think critically about the results.

When people in the organization see senior executives spending the time and mental energy to unpack the underlying assumptions that form the foundation for some proposed policy, practice, or intervention, they absorb a new cultural norm. The best leaders avoid the problem of seeming captious about the work of subordinates; they tap the collective wisdom and experience of their teams to explore whether assumptions seem sensible. They ask, "What would have to be true about people and organizations if this idea or practice were going to be effective? Does that feel true to us?"

Consultant claims may require an extra grain of salt. It is surprising how often purveyors of business knowledge are fooled or try to fool customers. We admire Bain & Company, for example, and believe it is quite capable of good research. We do wonder, however, why the company has a table on its Web site's home page that brags, "Our clients outperform the market 4 to 1" (the claim was "3 to 1" a few years back). The smart people at Bain know this correlation doesn't prove that their advice transformed clients into top performers. It could simply be that top performers have more money for hiring consultants. Indeed, any claim that Bain deserves credit for such performance is conspicuously absent from the Web site, at least as of fall 2005. Perhaps the

Are You Part of the Problem?

PERHAPS THE GREATEST BARRIER TO evidence-based management is that today's prevailing standards for assessing management knowledge are deeply flawed. Unfortunately, they are bolstered by the actions of virtually every major player in the marketplace for business knowledge. The business press in particular, purveyor of so many practices, needs to make better judgments about the virtues and shortcomings of the evidence it generates and publishes. We propose six standards for producing, evaluating, selling, and applying business knowledge.

1. Stop treating old ideas as if they were brand-new. Sir Isaac Newton is often credited as saying, "If I have seen farther, it is by standing on the shoulders of giants." But peddlers of management ideas find they win more speaking engagements and lucrative book contracts if they ignore antecedents and represent insights as being wholly original. Most business magazines happily recycle and rename concepts to keep the money flowing. This continues to happen even though, as renowned management theorist James March pointed out to us in an e-mail message, "most claims of originality are testimony to ignorance and most claims of magic are testimony to hubris." How do we break the cycle? For starters, people who spread ideas ought to acknowledge key sources and encourage writers and managers to build on and blend with what's come before. Doing so isn't just intellectually honest and polite. It leads to better ideas.

2. Be suspicious of "breakthrough" ideas and studies. Related to the desire for "new" is the desire for "big"—the big idea, the big study, the big innovation. Unfortunately, "big" rarely happens. Close examination of so-called breakthroughs nearly always reveals that they're preceded by the painstaking, incremental work of others. We live in a world where scientists and economists who win the Nobel Prize credit their predecessors' work; they carefully point out the tiny, excruciating steps they took over the years to develop their ideas and hesitate to declare breakthroughs, while—like old-fashioned snake oil salesmen—one business guru after another claims to have developed a brand-new cure-all. Something is wrong with this picture. Still, managers yearn for magic remedies, and purveyors pretend to give them what they crave.

3. Celebrate and develop collective brilliance. The business world is among the few places where the term "guru" has primarily positive connotations. But a focus on gurus masks how business knowledge is and ought to be developed and used. Knowledge is rarely generated by lone geniuses who cook up brilliant new ideas in their gigantic brains. Writers and consultants need to be more careful about describing the teams and communities of researchers who develop ideas. Even more important, they need to recognize that implementing practices, executing strategy, and accomplishing organizational change all require the coordinated actions of many people, whose commitment to an idea is greatest when they feel ownership.

4. Emphasize drawbacks as well as virtues. Doctors are getting better at explaining risks to patients and, in the best circumstances, enabling them to join a decision process where potential problems are considered. This rarely happens in management, where too many solutions are presented as costless and universally applicable, with little acknowledgment of possible pitfalls. Yet all management practices and programs have both strong and weak points, and even the best have costs. This doesn't mean companies shouldn't implement things like Six Sigma or Balanced Scorecards, just that they should recognize the hazards. That way, managers won't become disenchanted or, worse, abandon a valuable program or practice when known setbacks occur.

5. Use success (and failure) stories to illustrate sound practices, but not in place of a valid research method. There is an enormous problem with research that relies on recollection by the parties involved in a project, as so much management research does when it seeks out keys to subsequent success. A century ago, Ambrose Bierce, in his *Devil's Dictionary*, defined "recollect" as "To recall with additions something not previously known," foreshadowing

(continued)

99

much research on human memory. It turns out that, for example, eyewitness accounts are notoriously unreliable and that, in general, people have terrible memory, regardless of how confident they are in their recollections. Most relevant to management research is that people tend to remember much different things when they are anointed winners (versus losers), and what they recall has little to do with what happened.

6. Adopt a neutral stance toward ideologies and theories. Ideology is among the more widespread, potent, and vexing impediments to using evidence-based management. Academics and other thought leaders can come to believe in their own theories so fervently that they're incapable of learning from new evidence. And managers can lower or raise the threshold of their skepticism when a proposed solution, on its face, seems "vaguely socialistic" or "compassionate," "militaristic" or "disciplined." The best way to keep such filters from obscuring good solutions is to establish clarity and consensus on the problem to be solved and on what constitutes evidence of efficacy.

hope is that visitors will momentarily forget what they learned in their statistics classes!

Treat the Organization as an Unfinished Prototype

For some questions in some businesses, the best evidence is to be found at home—in the company's own data and experience rather than in the broader-based research of scholars. Companies that want to promote more evidence-based management should get in the habit of running trial programs, pilot studies, and small experiments, and thinking about the inferences that can be drawn from them, as CEO Gary Loveman has done at

Harrah's. Loveman joked to us that there are three ways to get fired at Harrah's these days: steal, harass women, or institute a program without first running an experiment. As you might expect, Harrah's experimentation is richest and most renowned in the area of marketing, where the company makes use of the data stream about customers' behaviors and responses to promotions. In one experiment reported by Harvard's Rajiv Lal in a teaching case, Harrah's offered a control group a promotional package worth $125 (a free room, two steak dinners, and $30 in casino chips); it offered customers in an experimental group just $60 in chips. The $60 offer generated more gambling revenue than the $125 offer did, and at a reduced cost. Loveman wanted to see experimentation like this throughout the business, not just in marketing. And so the company proved that spending money on employee selection and retention efforts (including giving people realistic job previews, enhancing training, and bolstering the quality of front-line supervision) would reduce turnover and produce more engaged and committed employees. Harrah's succeeded in reducing staff turnover by almost 50%.

Similarly, CEO Meg Whitman attributes much of eBay's success to the fact that management spends less time on strategic analysis and more time trying and tweaking things that seem like they might work. As she said in March 2005, "This is a completely new business, so there's only so much analysis you can do." Whitman suggests instead, "It's better to put something out there and see the reaction and fix it on the fly. You could spend six months getting it perfect in the lab . . . [but]

we're better off spending six days putting it out there, getting feedback, and then evolving it."

Yahoo is especially systematic about treating its home page as an unfinished prototype. Usama Fayyad, the company's chief data officer, points out that the home page gets millions of hits an hour, so Yahoo can conduct rigorous experiments that yield results in an hour or less—randomly assigning, say, a couple hundred thousand visitors to the experimental group and several million to the control group. Yahoo typically has 20 or so experiments running at any time, manipulating site features like colors, placement of advertisements, and location of text and buttons. These little experiments can have big effects. For instance, an experiment by data-mining researcher Nitin Sharma revealed that simply moving the search box from the side to the center of the home page would produce enough additional "click throughs" to bring in millions more dollars in advertising revenue a year.

A big barrier to using experiments to build management knowledge is that companies tend to adopt practices in an all-or-nothing way—either the CEO is behind the practice, so everyone does it or at least claims to, or it isn't tried at all. This tendency to do things everywhere or nowhere severely limits a company's ability to learn. In particular, multisite organizations like restaurants, hotels, and manufacturers with multiple locations can learn by experimenting in selected sites and making comparisons with "control" locations. Field experiments at places such as McDonald's restaurants, 7-Eleven convenience stores, Hewlett-Packard, and Intel have introduced changes in some units and not others to test the effects of different incentives, technologies, more interesting job content, open versus closed offices, and even detailed and warm (versus cursory and cold) explanations about why pay cuts were being implemented.

Embrace the attitude of wisdom

Something else, something broader, is more important than any single guideline for reaping the benefits of evidence-based management: the attitude people have toward business knowledge. At least since Plato's time, people have appreciated that true wisdom does not come from the sheer accumulation of knowledge, but from a healthy respect for and curiosity about the vast realms of knowledge still unconquered. Evidence-based management is conducted best not by know-it-alls but by managers who profoundly appreciate how much they do not know. These managers aren't frozen into inaction by ignorance; rather, they act on the best of their knowledge while questioning what they know.

Cultivating the right balance of humility and decisiveness is a huge, amorphous goal, but one tactic that serves it is to support the continuing professional education of managers with a commitment equal to that in other professions. The Centre for Evidence-Based Medicine says that identifying and applying effective strategies for lifelong learning are the keys to making this happen for physicians. The same things are surely critical to evidence-based management.

Another tactic is to encourage inquiry and observation even when rigorous evidence is lacking and you feel compelled to act quickly. If there is little or no information and you can't conduct a rigorous study, there are still things you can do to act more on the basis of logic and less on guesswork, fear, belief, or hope. We once worked with a large computer company that was having trouble selling its computers at retail stores. Senior executives kept blaming their marketing and sales staff for doing a bad job and dismissed complaints that it was hard to get customers to buy a lousy product—until one weekend, when members of the senior team went out to stores and tried to buy their computers. All of the executives encountered sales clerks who tried to dissuade them from buying the firm's computers, citing the excessive price, weak feature set, clunky appearance, and poor customer service. By organizing such field trips and finding other ways to gather qualitative data, managers can convey that decisions should not ignore real-world observations.

Will It Make a Difference?

The evidence-based-medicine movement has its critics, especially physicians who worry that clinical judgment will be replaced by search engines or who fear that bean counters from HMOs will veto experimental or expensive techniques. But initial studies suggest that physicians trained in evidence-based techniques are better informed than their peers, even 15 years after graduating from medical school. Studies also show conclusively that patients receiving the care that is indicated by evidence-based medicine experience better outcomes.

At this time, that level of assurance isn't available to those who undertake evidence-based management in business settings. We have the experience of relatively few companies to go on, and while it is positive, evidence from broad and representative samples is needed before that experience can be called a consistent pattern. Yet the theoretical argument strikes us as iron-clad. It seems perfectly logical that decisions made on the basis of a preponderance of evidence about what works elsewhere, as well as within your own company, will be better decisions and will help the organization thrive. We also have a huge body of peer-reviewed studies—literally thousands of careful studies by well-trained researchers—that, although routinely ignored, provide simple and powerful advice about how to run organizations. If found and used, this advice would have an immediate positive effect on organizations.

Does all this sound too obvious? Perhaps. But one of the most important lessons we've learned over the years is that practicing evidence-based management often entails being a master of the mundane. Consider how the findings from this one little study could help a huge organization: An experiment at the University of Missouri compared decision-making groups that stood up during ten- to 20-minute meetings with groups that sat down. Those that stood up took 34% less time to make decisions, and the quality was just as good. Whether people should sit down or stand up during meetings may seem a downright silly question at first blush. But do the math. Take energy giant Chevron, which has over 50,000 employees. If each employee replaced just one 20-minute sit-down meeting per year with a stand-up meeting, each of those meetings would be about seven minutes shorter. That would save Chevron over 350,000 minutes—nearly 6,000 hours— per year.

Leaders who are committed to practicing evidence-based management also need to brace themselves for a nasty side effect: When it is done right, it will undermine their power and prestige, which may prove unsettling to those who enjoy wielding influence. A former student of ours who worked at Netscape recalled a sentiment he'd once heard from James Barksdale back when he was CEO: "If the decision is going to be made by the facts, then everyone's facts, as long as they are relevant, are equal. If the decision is going to be made on the basis of people's opinions, then mine count for a lot more." This anecdote illustrates that facts and evidence are great levelers of hierarchy. Evidence-based practice changes power dynamics, replacing formal authority, reputation, and intuition with data. This means that senior leaders—often venerated for their wisdom and decisiveness—may lose some stature as their intuitions are replaced, at least at times, by judgments based on data available to virtually any educated person. The implication is that leaders need to make a fundamental decision: Do they want to be told they are always right, or do they want to lead organizations that actually perform well?

If taken seriously, evidence-based management can change how every manager thinks and acts. It is, first and foremost, a way of seeing the world and thinking about the craft of management; it proceeds from the premise that using better, deeper logic and employing facts, to the extent possible, permits leaders to do their jobs more effectively. We believe that facing the hard facts and truth about what works and what doesn't, understanding the dangerous half-truths that constitute so much conventional wisdom about management, and rejecting the total nonsense that too often passes for sound advice will help organizations perform better.

JEFFREY PFEFFER is the Thomas D. Dee II Professor of Organizational Behavior at Stanford Graduate School of Business. **ROBERT I. SUTTON** is a professor of management science and engineering at Stanford School of Engineering.

Originally published in January 2006. Reprint R0601E

What You Don't Know About Making Decisions

by David A. Garvin and Michael A. Roberto

LEADERS SHOW THEIR METTLE IN many ways—setting strategy and motivating people, just to mention two—but above all else leaders are made or broken by the quality of their decisions. That's a given, right? If you answered yes, then you would probably be surprised by how many executives approach decision making in a way that neither puts enough options on the table nor permits sufficient evaluation to ensure that they can make the best choice. Indeed, our research over the past several years strongly suggests that, simply put, most leaders get decision making all wrong.

The reason: Most businesspeople treat decision making as an event—a discrete choice that takes place at a single point in time, whether they're sitting at a desk, moderating a meeting, or staring at a spreadsheet. This classic view of decision making has a pronouncement popping out of a leader's head, based on experience, gut, research, or all three. Say the matter at hand is whether to pull a product with weak sales off the market. An "event" leader would mull in solitude, ask for advice, read reports, mull some more, then say yea or nay and send the organization off to make it happen. But to look at decision making that way is to overlook larger social and organizational contexts, which ultimately determine the success of any decision.

The fact is, decision making is not an event. It's a process, one that unfolds over weeks, months, or even years; one that's fraught with power plays and politics and is replete with personal nuances and institutional history; one that's rife with discussion and debate; and one that requires support at all levels of the organization when it comes time for execution. Our research shows that the difference between leaders who make good decisions and those who make bad ones is striking. The former recognize that all decisions are processes, and they explicitly design and manage them as such. The latter persevere in the fantasy that decisions are events they alone control.

In the following pages, we'll explore how leaders can design and manage a sound, effective decision-making process—an approach we call inquiry—and outline a set of criteria for assessing the quality of the decision-making process. First, a look at the process itself.

Decisions as Process: Inquiry Versus Advocacy

Not all decision-making processes are equally effective, particularly in the degree to which they allow a group to identify and consider a wide range of ideas. In our

Idea in Brief

The quality of a leader's decisions can make or break him. Yet most of us get decision making all wrong. Why? We take the least productive approach: **advocacy**. We argue our position with a passion that prevents us from weighing opposing views. We downplay our position's weaknesses to boost our chances of "winning." And we march into decision-making discussions armed for a battle of wills. The consequences? Fractious exchanges that discourage innovative thinking and stifle diverse, valuable viewpoints.

Contrast advocacy with **inquiry**—a much more productive decision-making approach. With inquiry, you carefully consider a variety of options, work with others to discover the best solutions, and stimulate creative thinking rather than suppressing dissension. The payoff? High-quality decisions that advance your company's objectives, and that you reach in a timely manner and implement effectively.

Inquiry isn't easy. You must promote constructive conflict and accept ambiguity. You also must balance *divergence* during early discussions with *unity* during implementation.

How to accomplish this feat? Master the "three C's" of decision making: **conflict, consideration,** and **closure**.

research, we've seen two broad approaches. *Inquiry,* which we prefer, is a very open process designed to generate multiple alternatives, foster the exchange of ideas, and produce a well-tested solution. Unfortunately, this approach doesn't come easily or naturally to most people. Instead, groups charged with making a decision tend to default to the second mode, one we call *advocacy.* The two look deceptively similar on the surface: groups of people, immersed in discussion and debate, trying to select a course of action by drawing on what they believe is the best available evidence. But despite their similarities, inquiry and advocacy produce dramatically different results.

Idea in Practice

Constructive Conflict

Conflict during decision making takes two forms: *cognitive* (relating to the substance of the work) and *affective* (stemming from interpersonal friction). The first is crucial to effective decision making; the second, destructive. To increase cognitive conflict while decreasing affective:

- **Require vigorous debate.** As a rule, ask tough questions and expect well-framed responses. Pose unexpected theoretical questions that stimulate productive thinking.

- **Prohibit language that triggers defensiveness.** Preface contradictory remarks or questions with phrases that remove blame and fault. ("Your arguments make good sense, but let me play devil's advocate for a moment.")

- **Break up natural coalitions.** Assign people to tasks without consideration of traditional loyalties. Require people with different interests to work together.

- **Shift individuals out of well-worn grooves.** During decision making, ask people to play functional or managerial roles different from their own; for example, lower-level employees assume a CEO's perspective.

- **Challenge stalemated participants to revisit key information.** Ask them to examine underlying assumptions and gather more facts.

Consideration

To gain your team's acceptance and support of a decision-making outcome—even if you've rejected their recommendations—ensure that they perceive the decision-making process as fair. How? Demonstrate consideration throughout the process:

- At the outset, **convey openness** to new ideas and willingness to accept differ-

When a group takes an advocacy perspective, participants approach decision making as a contest, although they don't necessarily compete openly or even consciously. Well-defined groups with special interests—dueling divisions in search of budget increases, for

ent views. Avoid indicating you've already made up your mind.

- During the discussion, **listen attentively**. Make eye contact and show patience while others explain their positions. Take notes, ask questions, and probe for deeper explanations.

- Afterward, **explain the rationale behind your decision**. Detail the criteria you used to select a course of action. Spell out how each participant's arguments affected the final decision.

Closure

In addition to stimulating constructive conflict and showing consideration, bring the decision process to closure at the appropriate time. Watch for two problems:

- **Deciding too early.** Worried about being dissenters, decision participants may readily accept the first plausible option rather than thoughtfully analyzing options. Unstated objections surface later—preventing cooperative action during the crucial implementation stage.

Watch for latent discontent in body language—furrowed brows, crossed arms, the curled-up posture of defiance. Call for a break, encourage each dissenter to speak up, then reconvene. Seek input from people known for raising hard questions and offering fresh perspectives.

- **Deciding too late.** Warring factions face off, restating their positions repeatedly. Or, striving for fairness, people insist on hearing every view and resolving every question before reaching closure.

To escape these endless loops, announce a decision. Accept that the decision-making process is ambiguous and that you'll never have complete, unequivocal data.

example—advocate for particular positions. Participants are passionate about their preferred solutions and therefore stand firm in the face of disagreement. That level of passion makes it nearly impossible to remain objective, limiting people's ability to pay attention to opposing

---

Two approaches to decision making

	Advocacy	Inquiry
Concept of decision making	a contest	collaborative problem solving
Purpose of discussion	persuasion and lobbying	testing and evaluation
Participants' role	spokespeople	critical thinkers
Patterns of behavior	strive to persuade others defend your position downplay weaknesses	present balanced arguments remain open to alternatives accept constructive criticism
Minority views	discouraged or dismissed	cultivated and valued
Outcome	winners and losers	collective ownership

---

arguments. Advocates often present information selectively, buttressing their arguments while withholding relevant conflicting data. Their goal, after all, is to make a compelling case, not to convey an evenhanded or balanced view. Two different plant managers pushing their own improvement programs, for example, may be wary of reporting potential weak points for fear that full disclosure will jeopardize their chances of winning the debate and gaining access to needed resources.

What's more, the disagreements that arise are frequently fractious and even antagonistic. Personalities and egos come into play, and differences are normally resolved through battles of wills and behind-the-scenes maneuvering. The implicit assumption is that a superior solution will emerge from a test of strength among competing positions. But in fact this approach typically suppresses innovation and encourages participants to go along with the dominant view to avoid further conflict.

By contrast, an inquiry-focused group carefully considers a variety of options and works together to discover the best solution. While people naturally continue to have their own interests, the goal is not to persuade the group to adopt a given point of view but instead to come to agreement on the best course of action. People share information widely, preferably in raw form, to allow participants to draw their own conclusions. Rather than suppressing dissension, an inquiry process encourages critical thinking. All participants feel comfortable raising alternative solutions and asking hard questions about the possibilities already on the table.

People engaged in an inquiry process rigorously question proposals and the assumptions they rest on, so conflict may be intense—but it is seldom personal. In fact, because disagreements revolve around ideas and interpretations rather than entrenched positions, conflict is generally healthy, and team members resolve their differences by applying rules of reason. The implicit assumption is that a consummate solution will emerge from a test of strength among competing ideas rather than dueling positions. Recent accounts of GE's succession process describe board members pursuing just such an open-minded approach. All members met repeatedly with the major candidates and gathered regularly to review their strengths and weaknesses—frequently without Jack Welch in attendance—with little or no attempt to lobby early for a particular choice.

A process characterized by inquiry rather than advocacy tends to produce decisions of higher quality—decisions that not only advance the company's objectives but also are reached in a timely manner and can be implemented effectively. Therefore, we believe that leaders seeking to improve their organizations' decision-making capabilities need to begin with a single goal: moving as quickly as possible from a process of advocacy to one of inquiry. That requires careful attention to three critical factors, the "three C's" of effective decision making: *conflict, consideration,* and *closure.* Each entails a delicate balancing act.

Constructive Conflict

Critical thinking and rigorous debate invariably lead to conflict. The good news is that conflict brings issues into focus, allowing leaders to make more informed choices. The bad news is that the wrong kind of conflict can derail the decision-making process altogether.

Indeed, conflict comes in two forms—*cognitive* and *affective.* Cognitive, or substantive, conflict relates to the work at hand. It involves disagreements over ideas and assumptions and differing views on the best way to proceed. Not only is such conflict healthy, it's crucial to effective inquiry. When people express differences openly and challenge underlying assumptions, they can flag real weaknesses and introduce new ideas. Affective, or interpersonal, conflict is emotional. It involves personal friction, rivalries, and clashing personalities, and it tends to diminish people's willingness to cooperate during implementation, rendering the decision-making process less effective. Not surprisingly, it is a common feature of advocacy processes.

On examination, the two are easy to distinguish. When a team member recalls "tough debates about the strategic, financial, and operating merits of the three acquisition candidates," she is referring to cognitive conflict. When a team member comments on "heated arguments that degenerated into personal attacks," he means affective conflict. But in practice the two types of conflict are surprisingly hard to separate. People tend to take any criticism personally and react defensively. The atmosphere quickly becomes charged, and even if a high-quality decision emerges, the emotional fallout tends to linger, making it hard for team members to work together during implementation.

The challenge for leaders is to increase cognitive conflict while keeping affective conflict low—no mean feat. One technique is to establish norms that make vigorous debate the rule rather than the exception. Chuck Knight, for 27 years the CEO of Emerson Electric, accomplished this by relentlessly grilling managers during planning reviews, no matter what he actually thought of the proposal on the table, asking tough, combative questions and expecting well-framed responses. The process— which Knight called the "logic of illogic" because of his willingness to test even well-crafted arguments by raising unexpected, and occasionally fanciful, concerns— was undoubtedly intimidating. But during his tenure it produced a steady stream of smart investment decisions and an unbroken string of quarterly increases in net income.

Bob Galvin, when he was CEO of Motorola in the 1980s, took a slightly different approach. He habitually asked unexpected hypothetical questions that stimulated creative thinking. Subsequently, as chairman of the board of overseers for the Malcolm Baldrige National Quality Program, Galvin took his colleagues by surprise when, in response to pressure from constituents to broaden the criteria for the award, he proposed narrowing them instead. In the end, the board did in fact broaden the criteria, but his seemingly out-of-the-blue suggestion sparked a creative and highly productive debate.

Another technique is to structure the conversation so that the process, by its very nature, fosters debate. This can be done by dividing people into groups with different, and often competing, responsibilities. For example, one group may be asked to develop a proposal while the other generates alternative recommendations. Then the groups would exchange proposals and discuss the various options. Such techniques virtually guarantee high levels of cognitive conflict. (The exhibit "Structuring the Debate" outlines two approaches for using different groups to stimulate creative thinking.)

But even if you've structured the process with an eye toward encouraging cognitive conflict, there's always a risk that it will become personal. Beyond cooling the debate with "time-outs," skilled leaders use a number of creative techniques to elevate cognitive debate while minimizing affective conflict.

Structuring the debate

By breaking a decision-making body into two subgroups, leaders can often create an environment in which people feel more comfortable engaging in debate. Scholars recommend two techniques in particular, which we call the "point-counterpoint" and "intellectual watchdog" approaches. The first three steps are the same for both techniques:

Point-counterpoint	Intellectual watchdog
The team divides into two subgroups.	The team divides into two subgroups.
Subgroup A develops a proposal, fleshing out the recommendation, the key assumptions, and the critical supporting data.	Subgroup A develops a proposal, fleshing out the recommendation, the key assumptions, and the critical supporting data.
Subgroup A presents the proposal to Subgroup B in written and oral forms.	Subgroup A presents the proposal to Subgroup B in written and oral forms.
Subgroup B generates one or more alternative plans of action.	Subgroup B develops a detailed critique of these assumptions and recommendations. It presents this critique in written and oral forms. Subgroup A revises its proposal based on this feedback.
The subgroups come together to debate the proposals and seek agreement on a common set of assumptions.	The subgroups continue in this revision-critique-revision cycle until they converge on a common set of assumptions.
Based on those assumptions, the subgroups continue to debate various options and strive to agree on a common set of recommendations.	Then, the subgroups work together to develop a common set of recommendations.

First, adroit leaders pay careful attention to the way issues are framed, as well as to the language used during discussions. They preface contradictory remarks or questions with phrases that remove some of the personal sting ("Your arguments make good sense, but let me play devil's advocate for a moment"). They also set ground rules about language, insisting that team members avoid words and behavior that trigger defensiveness. For instance, in the U.S. Army's after-action reviews, conducted immediately after missions to identify mistakes so they can be avoided next time, facilitators make a point of saying, "We don't use the 'b' word, and we don't use the 'f' word. We don't place blame, and we don't find fault."

Second, leaders can help people step back from their preestablished positions by breaking up natural coalitions and assigning people to tasks on some basis other than traditional loyalties. At a leading aerospace company, one business unit president had to deal with two powerful coalitions within his organization during a critical decision about entering into a strategic alliance. When he set up two groups to consider alternative alliance partners, he interspersed the groups with members of each coalition, forcing people with different interests to work with one another. He then asked both groups to evaluate the same wide range of options using different criteria (such as technological capability, manufacturing prowess, or project management skills). The two groups then shared their evaluations and worked together to select the best partner. Because nobody had complete information, they were forced to listen closely to one another.

Third, leaders can shift individuals out of well-grooved patterns, where vested interests are highest.

They can, for example, ask team members to research and argue for a position they did not endorse during initial discussions. Similarly, they can assign team members to play functional or managerial roles different from their own, such as asking an operations executive to take the marketing view or asking a lower-level employee to assume the CEO's strategic perspective.

Finally, leaders can ask participants locked in debate to revisit key facts and assumptions and gather more information. Often, people become so focused on the differences between opposing positions that they reach a stalemate. Emotional conflict soon follows. Asking people to examine underlying presumptions can defuse the tension and set the team back on track. For instance, at Enron, when people disagree strongly about whether or not to apply their trading skills to a new commodity or market, senior executives quickly refocus the discussion on characteristics of industry structure and assumptions about market size and customer preferences. People quickly recognize areas of agreement, discover precisely how and why they disagree, and then focus their debate on specific issues.

Consideration

Once a decision's been made and the alternatives dismissed, some people will have to surrender the solution they preferred. At times, those who are overruled resist the outcome; at other times, they display grudging acceptance. What accounts for the difference? The critical factor appears to be the perception of fairness—what

Advocacy Versus Inquiry in Action: The Bay of Pigs and the Cuban Missile Crisis

PERHAPS THE BEST DEMONSTRATION OF advocacy versus inquiry comes from the administration of President John F. Kennedy. During his first two years in office, Kennedy wrestled with two critical foreign policy decisions: the Bay of Pigs invasion and the Cuban Missile Crisis. Both were assigned to cabinet-level task forces, involving many of the same players, the same political interests, and extremely high stakes. But the results were extraordinarily different, largely because the two groups operated in different modes.

The first group, charged with deciding whether to support an invasion of Cuba by a small army of U.S.-trained Cuban exiles, worked in advocacy mode, and the outcome is widely regarded as an example of flawed decision making. Shortly after taking office, President Kennedy learned of the planned attack on Cuba developed by the CIA during the Eisenhower administration. Backed by the Joint Chiefs of Staff, the CIA argued forcefully for the invasion and minimized the risks, filtering the information presented to the president to reinforce the agency's position. Knowledgeable individuals on the State Department's Latin America desk were excluded from deliberations because of their likely opposition.

Some members of Kennedy's staff opposed the plan but held their tongues for fear of appearing weak in the face of strong advocacy by the CIA. As a result, there was little debate, and the group failed to test some critical underlying assumptions. For example, they didn't question whether the landing would in fact lead to a rapid domestic uprising against Castro, and they failed to find out whether the exiles could fade into the mountains (which were 80 miles from the landing site) should they meet with strong resistance. The resulting invasion is generally considered to be one of the low points of the Cold War. About 100 lives were lost, and the rest of the exiles were taken hostage. The incident was a major embarrassment to the Kennedy administration and dealt a blow to America's global standing.

After the botched invasion, Kennedy conducted a review of the foreign policy decision-making process and introduced five major changes, essentially transforming the process into one of inquiry. First, people were urged to participate in discussions as "skeptical generalists"—that is, as disinterested critical thinkers rather than as representatives of particular departments. Second, Robert Kennedy and Theodore Sorensen were assigned the role of intellectual watchdog, expected to pursue every possible point of contention, uncovering weaknesses and untested assumptions. Third, task forces were urged to abandon the rules of protocol, eliminating formal agendas and deference to rank. Fourth, participants were expected to split occasionally into subgroups to develop a broad range of options. And finally, President Kennedy decided to absent himself from some of the early task force meetings to avoid influencing other participants and slanting the debate.

The inquiry mode was used to great effect when in October 1962 President Kennedy learned that the Soviet Union had placed nuclear missiles on Cuban soil, despite repeated assurances from the Soviet ambassador that this would not occur. Kennedy immediately convened a high-level task force, which contained many of the same men responsible for the Bay of Pigs invasion, and asked them to frame a response. The group met night and day for two weeks, often inviting additional members to join in their deliberations to broaden their perspective. Occasionally, to encourage the free flow of ideas, they met without the president. Robert Kennedy played his new role thoughtfully, critiquing options frequently and encouraging the group to develop additional alternatives. In particular, he urged the group to move beyond a simple go-no-go decision on a military air strike.

(continued)

Ultimately, subgroups developed two positions, one favoring a blockade and the other an air strike. These groups gathered information from a broad range of sources, viewed and interpreted the same intelligence photos, and took great care to identify and test underlying assumptions, such as whether the Tactical Air Command was indeed capable of eliminating all Soviet missiles in a surgical air strike. The subgroups exchanged position papers, critiqued each other's proposals, and came together to debate the alternatives. They presented Kennedy with both options, leaving him to make the final choice. The result was a carefully framed response, leading to a successful blockade and a peaceful end to the crisis.

scholars call "procedural justice." The reality is that the leader will make the ultimate decision, but the people participating in the process must believe that their views were considered and that they had a genuine opportunity to influence the final decision. Researchers have found that if participants believe the process was fair, they are far more willing to commit themselves to the resulting decision even if their views did not prevail. (For a detailed discussion of this phenomenon, see W. Chan Kim and Renée Mauborgne, "Fair Process: Managing in the Knowledge Economy," HBR July–August 1997).

Many managers equate fairness with *voice*—with giving everyone a chance to express his or her own views. They doggedly work their way around the table, getting everyone's input. However, voice is not nearly as important as *consideration*—people's belief that the leader actively listened to them during the discussions and weighed their views carefully before reaching a decision. In his 1999 book, *Only the Paranoid Survive,* Intel's chairman Andy Grove describes how he explains the distinction to his middle managers: "Your criterion for involvement should be that you're heard and understood. . . . All sides cannot prevail in the debate, but all opinions have value in shaping the right answer."

In fact, voice without consideration is often damaging; it leads to resentment and frustration rather than to acceptance. When the time comes to implement the decision, people are likely to drag their feet if they sense that the decision-making process had been a sham—an exercise in going through the motions designed to validate the leader's preferred solution. This appears to have been true of the Daimler-Chrysler merger. Daimler CEO Jurgen Schrempp asked for extensive analysis and assessment of potential merger candidates but had long before settled on Chrysler as his choice. In fact, when consultants told him that his strategy was unlikely to create shareholder value, he dismissed the data and went ahead with his plans. Schrempp may have solicited views from many parties, but he clearly failed to give them much weight.

Leaders can demonstrate consideration throughout the decision-making process. At the outset, they need to convey openness to new ideas and a willingness to accept views that differ from their own. In particular, they must avoid suggesting that their minds are already made up. They should avoid disclosing their personal preferences early in the process, or they should clearly state that any initial opinions are provisional and subject to change. Or they can absent themselves from early deliberations.

During the discussions, leaders must take care to show that they are listening actively and attentively. How? By asking questions, probing for deeper explanations, echoing comments, making eye contact, and showing patience when participants explain their positions. Taking notes is an especially powerful signal, since it suggests that the leader is making a real effort to capture, understand, and evaluate people's thoughts.

And after they make the final choice, leaders should explain their logic. They must describe the rationale for their decision, detailing the criteria they used to select a course of action. Perhaps more important, they need to convey how each participant's arguments affected the final decision or explain clearly why they chose to differ with those views.

Closure

Knowing when to end deliberations is tricky; all too often decision-making bodies rush to a conclusion or else dither endlessly and decide too late. Deciding too early is as damaging as deciding too late, and both problems can usually be traced to unchecked advocacy.

Deciding Too Early
Sometimes people's desire to be considered team players overrides their willingness to engage in critical thinking and thoughtful analysis, so the group readily accepts the first remotely plausible option. Popularly

known as "groupthink," this mind-set is prevalent in the presence of strong advocates, especially in new teams, whose members are still learning the rules and may be less willing to stand out as dissenters.

The danger of groupthink is not only that it suppresses the full range of options but also that unstated objections will come to the surface at some critical moment—usually at a time when aligned, cooperative action is essential to implementation. The leader of a large division of a fast-growing retailer learned this the hard way. He liked to work with a small subset of his senior team to generate options, evaluate the alternatives, and develop a plan of action, and then bring the proposal back to the full team for validation. At that point, his managers would feel they had been presented with a fait accompli and so would be reluctant to raise their concerns. As one of them put it: "Because the meeting is the wrong place to object, we don't walk out of the room as a unified group." Instead, they would reopen the debate during implementation, delaying important initiatives by many months.

As their first line of defense against group-think, leaders need to learn to recognize latent discontent, paying special attention to body language: furrowed brows, crossed arms, or curled-up defiance. To bring disaffected people back into the discussion, it may be best to call for a break, approach dissenters one by one, encourage them to speak up, and then reconvene. GM's Alfred Sloan was famous for this approach, which he would introduce with the following speech: "I take it we are all in complete agreement on the decision here.

Then I propose we postpone further discussion of the matter until our next meeting to give ourselves time to develop disagreement and perhaps gain some under-standing of what the decision is all about."

Another way to avoid early closure is to cultivate mi-nority views either through norms or through explicit rules. Minority views broaden and deepen debate; they stretch a group's thinking, even though they are seldom adopted intact. It is for this reason that Andy Grove routinely seeks input from "helpful Cassandras," people who are known for raising hard questions and offering fresh perspectives about the dangers of proposed policies.

Deciding Too Late

Here, too, unchecked advocacy is frequently the source of the problem, and in these instances it takes two main forms. At times, a team hits gridlock: Warring factions refuse to yield, restating their positions over and over again. Without a mechanism for breaking the deadlock, discussions become an endless loop. At other times, people bend over backward to ensure evenhanded par-ticipation. Striving for fairness, team members insist on hearing every view and resolving every question before reaching a conclusion. This demand for certainty—for complete arguments backed by unassailable data—is its own peculiar form of advocacy. Once again, the result is usually an endless loop, replaying the same alterna-tives, objections, and requests for further information. Any member of the group can unilaterally derail the dis-cussion by voicing doubts. Meanwhile, competitive pressures may be demanding an immediate response, or participants may have tuned out long ago, as the same arguments are repeated ad nauseam.

At this point, it's the leader's job to "call the question." Jamie Houghton, the longtime CEO of Corning, invented a vivid metaphor to describe this role. He spoke of wearing two hats when working with his senior team: He figuratively put on his cowboy hat when he wanted to debate with members as an equal, and he donned a bowler when, as CEO, he called the question and announced a decision. The former role allowed for challenges and continued discussion; the latter signaled an end to the debate.

The message here is that leaders—and their teams— need to become more comfortable with ambiguity and be willing to make speedy decisions in the absence of complete, unequivocal data or support. As Dean Stanley Teele of Harvard Business School was fond of telling students: "The art of management is the art of making meaningful generalizations out of inadequate facts."

A Litmus Test

Unfortunately, superior decision making is distressingly difficult to assess in real time. Successful outcomes— decisions of high quality, made in a timely manner and implemented effectively—can be evaluated only after the fact. But by the time the results are in, it's normally too late to take corrective action. Is there any way to find out earlier whether you're on the right track?

There is indeed. The trick, we believe, is to periodically assess the decision-making process, even as it is under way. Scholars now have considerable evidence showing that a small set of process traits is closely linked with superior outcomes. While they are no guarantee of success, their combined presence sharply improves the odds that you'll make a good decision.

Multiple Alternatives

When groups consider many alternatives, they engage in more thoughtful analysis and usually avoid settling too quickly on the easy, obvious answer. This is one reason techniques like point-counterpoint, which requires groups to generate at least two alternatives, are so often associated with superior decision making. Usually, keeping track of the number of options being considered will tell if this test has been met. But take care not to double count. Go-no-go choices involve only one option and don't qualify as two alternatives.

Assumption Testing

"Facts" come in two varieties: those that have been carefully tested and those that have been merely asserted or assumed. Effective decision-making groups do not confuse the two. They periodically step back from their arguments and try to confirm their assumptions by examining them critically. If they find that some still lack hard evidence, they may elect to proceed, but they will at least know they're venturing into uncertain territory. Alternatively, the group may designate "intellectual watchdogs" who are assigned the task of scrutinizing the process for unchecked assumptions and challenging them on the spot.

Well-Defined Criteria

Without crisp, clear goals, it's easy to fall into the trap of comparing apples with oranges. Competing arguments become difficult to judge, since advocates will suggest using those measures (net income, return on capital, market presence, share of mind, and so on) that favor their preferred alternative. Fuzzy thinking and long delays are the likely result.

To avoid the problem, the team should specify goals up front and revisit them repeatedly during the decision-making process. These goals can be complex and multifaceted, quantitative and qualitative, but whatever form they take, they must remain at the fore. Studies of merger decisions have found that as the process reaches its final stages and managers feel the pressure of deadlines and the rush to close, they often compromise or adjust the criteria they originally created for judging the appropriateness of the deal.

Dissent and Debate

David Hume, the great Scottish philosopher, argued persuasively for the merits of debate when he observed that the "truth springs from arguments amongst friends." There are two ways to measure the health of a debate: the kinds of questions being asked and the level of listening.

Some questions open up discussion; others narrow it and end deliberations. Contrarian hypothetical questions usually trigger healthy debate. A manager who worked for former American Express CEO Harvey Golub points to a time when the company was committed to lowering credit card fees, and Golub unexpectedly proposed raising fees instead. "I don't think he meant it seriously," says the manager. "But he certainly taught us how to think about fees."

The level of listening is an equally important indicator of a healthy decision-making process. Poor listening produces flawed analysis as well as personal friction. If participants routinely interrupt one another or pile on rebuttals before digesting the preceding comment, affective conflict is likely to materialize. Civilized discussions quickly become impossible, for collegiality and group harmony usually disappear in the absence of active listening.

Perceived Fairness

A real-time measure of perceived fairness is the level of participation that's maintained after a key midpoint or milestone has been reached. Often, a drop in participation is an early warning of problems with implementation since some members of the group are already showing their displeasure by voting with their feet.

In fact, keeping people involved in the process is, in the end, perhaps the most crucial factor in making a decision—and making it stick. It's a job that lies at the heart of leadership and one that uniquely combines the leader's numerous talents. It requires the fortitude to promote conflict while accepting ambiguity, the wisdom to know when to bring conversations to a close, the patience to help others understand the reasoning behind your choice, and, not least, a genius for balance—the ability to embrace both the divergence that may characterize early discussions and the unity needed for effective implementation. Cyrus the Great, the founder of the Persian Empire and a renowned military leader, understood the true hallmark of leadership in the sixth century bc, when he attributed his success to "diversity in counsel, unity in command."

DAVID A. GARVIN is the Robert and Jane Cizik Professor of Business Administration and **MICHAEL A. ROBERTO** is an assistant professor at Harvard Business School.

Originally published in August 2001. Reprint R0108G

Who Has the D?

How Clear Decision Roles Enhance Organizational Performance
by Paul Rogers and Marcia Blenko

DECISIONS ARE THE COIN OF the realm in business. Every success, every mishap, every opportunity seized or missed is the result of a decision that someone made or failed to make. At many companies, decisions routinely get stuck inside the organization like loose change. But it's more than loose change that's at stake, of course; it's the performance of the entire organization. Never mind what industry you're in, how big and well known your company may be, or how clever your strategy is. If you can't make the right decisions quickly and effectively, and execute those decisions consistently, your business will lose ground.

Indeed, making good decisions and making them happen quickly are the hallmarks of high-performing organizations. When we surveyed executives at 350 global companies about their organizational effectiveness, only 15% said that they have an organization that helps the business outperform competitors. What sets those top performers apart is the quality, speed, and execution of their decision making. The most effective organizations score well on the major strategic decisions—which markets to enter or exit, which businesses to buy or sell, where to allocate capital and talent. But they truly shine when it comes to the critical operating decisions requiring consistency and speed—how to drive product innovation, the best way to position brands, how to manage channel partners.

Even in companies respected for their decisiveness, however, there can be ambiguity over who is accountable for which decisions. As a result, the entire decision-making process can stall, usually at one of four bottlenecks: global versus local, center versus business unit, function versus function, and inside versus outside partners.

The first of these bottlenecks, *global versus local* decision making, can occur in nearly every major business process and function. Decisions about brand building and product development frequently get snared here, when companies wrestle over how much authority local businesses should have to tailor products for their markets. Marketing is another classic global versus local issue—should local markets have the power to determine pricing and advertising?

The second bottleneck, *center versus business unit* decision making, tends to afflict parent companies and their subsidiaries. Business units are on the front line, close to the customer; the center sees the big picture, sets broad goals, and keeps the organization focused on winning. Where should the decision-making power lie? Should a major capital investment, for example, depend

Idea in Brief

Decisions are the coin of the realm in business. Every success, every mishap, every opportunity seized or missed stems from a decision someone made—or failed to make. Yet in many firms, decisions routinely stall inside the organization—hurting the entire company's performance.

The culprit? Ambiguity over who's accountable for which decisions. In one auto manufacturer that was missing milestones for rolling out new models, marketers *and* product developers each thought they were responsible for deciding new models' standard features and colors. Result? Conflict over who had final say, endless revisiting of decisions—and missed deadlines that led to lost sales.

How to clarify decision accountability? Assign clear roles for the decisions that most affect your firm's performance—such as which markets to enter, where to allocate capital, and how to drive product innovation. Think "RAPID": Who should recommend a course of action on a key decision? Who must agree to a recommendation before it can move forward? Who will perform the actions needed to implement the decision? Whose input is needed to determine the proposal's feasibility? Who decides—brings the decision to closure and commits the organization to implement it?

When you clarify decision roles, you make the *right* choices—swiftly and effectively.

on the approval of the business unit that will own it, or should headquarters make the final call?

Function versus function decision making is perhaps the most common bottleneck. Every manufacturer, for instance, faces a balancing act between product development and marketing during the design of a new product. Who should decide what? Cross-functional decisions too often result in ineffective compromise solutions, which frequently need to be revisited because the right people were not involved at the outset.

Idea in Practice

The RAPID Decision Model
For every strategic decision, assign the following roles and responsibilities:

People who. . .	Are responsible for . . .
Recommend	• Making a proposal on a key decision, gathering input, and providing data and analysis to make a sensible choice in a timely fashion • Consulting with input providers—hearing and incorporating their views, and winning their buy-in
Agree	• Negotiating a modified proposal with the recommender if they have concerns about the original proposal • Escalating unresolved issues to the decider if the "A" and "R" can't resolve differences • If necessary, exercising veto power over the recommendation
Perform	• Executing a decision once it's made • Seeing that the decision is implemented promptly and effectively
Input	• Providing relevant facts to the recommender that shed light on the proposal's feasibility and practical implications
Decide	• Serving as the single point of accountability • Bringing the decision to closure by resolving any impasse in the decision-making process • Committing the organization to implementing the decision

The fourth decision-making bottleneck, *inside versus outside partners,* has become familiar with the rise of outsourcing, joint ventures, strategic alliances, and franchising. In such arrangements, companies need to be absolutely clear about which decisions can be

Decision-Role Pitfalls

In assigning decision roles:

- Ensure that only one person "has the D." If two or more people think they're in charge of a particular decision, a tug-of-war results.

- Watch for a proliferation of "A's." Too many people with veto power can paralyze recommenders. If many people must agree, you probably haven't pushed decisions down far enough in your organization.

- Avoid assigning too many "I's." When many people give input, at least some of them aren't making meaningful contributions.

The RAPID Model in Action

Example: At British department-store chain John Lewis, company buyers wanted to increase sales and reduce complexity by offering fewer salt and pepper mill models.

The company launched the streamlined product set without involving the sales staff. And sales fell. Upon visiting the stores, buyers saw that salespeople (not understanding the strategy behind the recommendation) had halved shelf space to match the reduction in product range, rather than maintaining the same space but stocking more of the products.

To fix the problem, the company "gave buyers the D" on how much space product categories would have. Sales staff "had the A": If space allocations didn't make sense to them, they could force additional negotiations. They also "had the P," implementing product layouts in stores.

Once decision roles were clarified, sales of salt and pepper mills exceeded original levels.

owned by the external partner (usually those about the execution of strategy) and which must continue to be made internally (decisions about the strategy itself). In the case of outsourcing, for instance, brand-name apparel and footwear marketers once assumed that overseas suppliers could be responsible for decisions about plant employees' wages and working conditions. Big mistake.

Clearing the Bottlenecks

The most important step in unclogging decision-making bottlenecks is assigning clear roles and responsibilities. Good decision makers recognize which decisions really matter to performance. They think through who should recommend a particular path, who needs to agree, who should have input, who has ultimate responsibility for making the decision, and who is accountable for follow-through. They make the process routine. The result: better coordination and quicker response times.

Companies have devised a number of methods to clarify decision roles and assign responsibilities. We have used an approach called RAPID, which has evolved over the years, to help hundreds of companies develop clear decision-making guidelines. It is, for sure, not a panacea (an indecisive decision maker, for example, can ruin any good system), but it's an important start. The letters in RAPID stand for the primary roles in any decision-making process, although these roles are not performed exactly in this order: recommend, agree, perform, input, and decide—the "D." (See the sidebar "A Decision-Making Primer.")

The people who *recommend* a course of action are responsible for making a proposal or offering alternatives. They need data and analysis to support their recommendations, as well as common sense about what's reasonable, practical, and effective.

The people who *agree* to a recommendation are those who need to sign off on it before it can move forward. If they veto a proposal, they must either work with the recommender to come up with an alternative or elevate the issue to the person with the D. For decision making to function smoothly, only a few people should have such veto power. They may be executives responsible for legal or regulatory compliance or the heads of units whose operations will be significantly affected by the decision.

People with *input* responsibilities are consulted about the recommendation. Their role is to provide the relevant facts that are the basis of any good decision: How practical is the proposal? Can manufacturing accommodate the design change? Where there's dissent or contrasting views, it's important to get these people to the table at the right time. The recommender has no obligation to act on the input he or she receives but is expected to take it into account—particularly since the people who provide input are generally among those who must implement a decision. Consensus is a worthy goal, but as a decision-making standard, it can be an obstacle to action or a recipe for lowest-common-denominator compromise. A more practical objective is to get everyone involved to buy in to the decision.

Eventually, one person will *decide*. The decision maker is the single point of accountability who must

A Decision-Making Primer

GOOD DECISION MAKING DEPENDS ON assigning clear and specific roles. This sounds simple enough, but many companies struggle to make decisions because lots of people feel accountable—or no one does. RAPID and other tools used to analyze decision making give senior management teams a method for assigning roles and involving the relevant people. The key is to be clear who has input, who gets to decide, and who gets it done.

The five letters in RAPID correspond to the five critical decision-making roles: recommend, agree, perform, input, and decide. As you'll see, the roles are not carried out lockstep in this order—we took some liberties for the sake of creating a useful acronym.

Recommend

People in this role are responsible for making a proposal, gathering input, and providing the right data and analysis to make a sensible decision in a timely fashion. In the course of developing a proposal, recommenders consult with the people who provide input, not just hearing and incorporating their views but also building buy in along the way. Recommenders must have analytical skills, common sense, and organizational smarts.

Agree

Individuals in this role have veto power—yes or no—over the recommendation. Exercising the veto triggers a debate between themselves and the recommenders, which should lead to a modified proposal. If that takes too long, or if the two parties simply can't agree, they can escalate the issue to the person who has the D.

Input

These people are consulted on the decision. Because the people who provide input are typically involved in implementation, recommenders have a strong interest in taking their advice seriously. No input is binding, but this shouldn't undermine its importance. If the right people are not involved and motivated, the decision is far more likely to falter during execution.

Decide

The person with the D is the formal decision maker. He or she is ultimately accountable for the decision, for better or worse, and has the authority to resolve any impasse in the decision-making process and to commit the organization to action.

Perform

Once a decision is made, a person or group of people will be responsible for executing it. In some instances, the people responsible for implementing a decision are the same people who recommended it.

Writing down the roles and assigning accountability are essential steps, but good decision making also requires the right process. Too many rules can cause the process to collapse under its own weight. The most effective process is grounded in specifics but simple enough to adapt if necessary.

When the process gets slowed down, the problem can often be traced back to one of three trouble spots. First is a lack of clarity about who has the D. If more than one person think they have it for a particular decision, that decision will get caught up in a tug-of-war. The flip side can be equally damaging: No one is accountable for crucial decisions, and the business suffers. Second, a proliferation of people who have veto power can make life tough for recommenders. If a company has too many people in the "agree" role, it usually means that decisions are not pushed down far enough in the organization. Third, if there are a lot of people giving input, it's a signal that at least some of them aren't making a meaningful contribution.

bring the decision to closure and commit the organization to act on it. To be strong and effective, the person with the D needs good business judgment, a grasp of the relevant trade-offs, a bias for action, and a keen awareness of the organization that will execute the decision.

The final role in the process involves the people who will *perform* the decision. They see to it that the decision is implemented promptly and effectively. It's a crucial role. Very often, a good decision executed quickly beats a brilliant decision implemented slowly or poorly.

RAPID can be used to help redesign the way an organization works or to target a single bottleneck. Some companies use the approach for the top ten to 20 decisions, or just for the CEO and his or her direct reports. Other companies use it throughout the organization— to improve customer service by clarifying decision roles on the front line, for instance. When people see an effective process for making decisions, they spread the word. For example, after senior managers at a major U.S. retailer used RAPID to sort out a particularly thorny set of corporate decisions, they promptly built the process into their own functional organizations.

To see the process in action, let's look at the way four companies have worked through their decision-making bottlenecks.

Global Versus Local

Every major company today operates in global markets, buying raw materials in one place, shipping them somewhere else, and selling finished products all over the world. Most are trying simultaneously to build local presence and expertise, and to achieve economies of scale. Decision making in this environment is far from straightforward. Frequently, decisions cut across the boundaries between global and local managers, and sometimes across a regional layer in between: What investments will streamline our supply chain? How far should we go in standardizing products or tailoring them for local markets?

The trick in decision making is to avoid becoming either mindlessly global or hopelessly local. If decision-making authority tilts too far toward global executives, local customers' preferences can easily be overlooked, undermining the efficiency and agility of local operations. But with too much local authority, a company is likely to miss out on crucial economies of scale or opportunities with global clients.

To strike the right balance, a company must recognize its most important sources of value and make sure that decision roles line up with them. This was the challenge facing Martin Broughton, the former CEO and chairman of British American Tobacco, the second-largest tobacco company in the world. In 1993, when Broughton was appointed chief executive, BAT was losing ground to its nearest competitor. Broughton knew that the company needed to take better advantage of its global scale, but decision roles and responsibilities were at odds with this goal. Four geographic operating units ran themselves autonomously, rarely collaborating and sometimes even competing. Achieving consistency across global brands proved difficult, and cost synergies across the operating units were elusive. Industry insiders joked that "there are seven major tobacco companies in the world—and four of them are British American Tobacco." Broughton vowed to change the punch line.

The chief executive envisioned an organization that could take advantage of the opportunities a global business offers—global brands that could compete with established winners such as Altria Group's Marlboro; global purchasing of important raw materials, including tobacco; and more consistency in innovation and customer management. But Broughton didn't want the company to lose its nimbleness and competitive hunger in local markets by shifting too much decision-making power to global executives.

The first step was to clarify roles for the most important decisions. Procurement became a proving ground. Previously, each operating unit had identified its own suppliers and negotiated contracts for all materials. Under Broughton, a global procurement team was set up in headquarters and given authority to choose suppliers and negotiate pricing and quality for global materials, including bulk tobacco and certain types of packaging. Regional procurement teams were now given input into global materials strategies but ultimately had to implement the team's decision. As soon as the global team signed contracts with suppliers, responsibility shifted to the regional teams, who worked out the details of delivery and service with the suppliers in their regions. For materials that did not offer global economies of scale (mentholated filters for the

North American market, for example), the regional teams retained their decision-making authority.

As the effort to revamp decision making in procurement gained momentum, the company set out to clarify roles in all its major decisions. The process wasn't easy. A company the size of British American Tobacco has a huge number of moving parts, and developing a practical system for making decisions requires sweating lots of details. What's more, decision-making authority is power, and people are often reluctant to give it up.

It's crucial for the people who will live with the new system to help design it. At BAT, Broughton created working groups led by people earmarked, implicitly or explicitly, for leadership roles in the future. For example, Paul Adams, who ultimately succeeded Broughton as chief executive, was asked to lead the group charged with redesigning decision making for brand and customer management. At the time, Adams was a regional head within one of the operating units. With other senior executives, including some of his own direct reports, Broughton specified that their role was to provide input, not to veto recommendations. Broughton didn't make the common mistake of seeking consensus, which is often an obstacle to action. Instead, he made it clear that the objective was not deciding whether to change the decision-making process but achieving buy in about how to do so as effectively as possible.

The new decision roles provided the foundation the company needed to operate successfully on a global basis while retaining flexibility at the local level. The focus and efficiency of its decision making were reflected in the company's results: After the decision-making overhaul, British American Tobacco experienced nearly ten years of growth well above the levels of its competitors in sales, profits, and market value. The company has gone on to have one of the best-performing stocks on the UK market and has reemerged as a major global player in the tobacco industry.

Center Versus Business Unit

The first rule for making good decisions is to involve the right people at the right level of the organization. For BAT, capturing economies of scale required its global team to appropriate some decision-making powers from regional divisions. For many companies, a similar balancing act takes place between executives at the center and managers in the business units. If too many decisions flow to the center, decision making can grind to a halt. The problem is different but no less critical if the decisions that are elevated to senior executives are the wrong ones.

Companies often grow into this type of problem. In small and midsize organizations, a single management team—sometimes a single leader—effectively handles every major decision. As a company grows and its operations become more complex, however, senior executives can no longer master the details required to make decisions in every business.

A change in management style, often triggered by the arrival of a new CEO, can create similar tensions. At a large British retailer, for example, the senior team was accustomed to the founder making all critical decisions. When his successor began seeking consensus on important issues, the team was suddenly unsure of its role, and many decisions stalled. It's a common scenario, yet most management teams and boards of directors don't specify how decision-making authority should change as the company does.

A growth opportunity highlighted that issue for Wyeth (then known as American Home Products) in late 2000. Through organic growth, acquisitions, and partnerships, Wyeth's pharmaceutical division had developed three sizable businesses: biotech, vaccines, and traditional pharmaceutical products. Even though each business had its own market dynamics, operating requirements, and research focus, most important decisions were pushed up to one group of senior executives. "We were using generalists across all issues," said Joseph M. Mahady, president of North American and global businesses for Wyeth Pharmaceuticals. "It was a signal that we weren't getting our best decision making."

The problem crystallized for Wyeth when managers in the biotech business saw a vital—but perishable— opportunity to establish a leading position with Enbrel, a promising rheumatoid arthritis drug. Competitors were working on the same class of drug, so Wyeth needed to move quickly. This meant expanding production capacity by building a new plant, which would be located at the Grange Castle Business Park in Dublin, Ireland.

The decision, by any standard, was a complex one. Once approved by regulators, the facility would be the biggest biotech plant in the world—and the largest capital investment Wyeth had ever undertaken. Yet peak demand for the drug was not easy to determine. What's more, Wyeth planned to market Enbrel in partnership with Immunex (now a part of Amgen). In its deliberations about the plant, therefore, Wyeth needed to factor in the requirements of building up its technical expertise, technology transfer issues, and an uncertain competitive environment.

Input on the decision filtered up slowly through a gauze of overlapping committees, leaving senior executives hungry for a more detailed grasp of the issues. Given the narrow window of opportunity, Wyeth acted quickly, moving from a first look at the Grange Castle project to implementation in six months. But in the midst of this process, Wyeth Pharmaceuticals' executives saw the larger issue: The company needed a system that would push more decisions down to the business units, where operational knowledge was greatest, and elevate the decisions that required the senior team's input, such as marketing strategy and manufacturing capacity.

In short order, Wyeth gave authority for many decisions to business unit managers, leaving senior executives with veto power over some of the more sensitive issues related to Grange Castle. But after that investment decision was made, the D for many subsequent decisions about the Enbrel business lay with Cavan Redmond, the executive vice president and general manager of Wyeth's biotech division, and his new management team. Redmond gathered input from managers in biotech manufacturing, marketing, forecasting, finance, and R&D, and quickly set up the complex schedules needed to collaborate with Immunex. Responsibility for execution rested firmly with the business unit, as always. But now Redmond, supported by his team, also had authority to make important decisions.

Grange Castle is paying off so far. Enbrel is among the leading brands for rheumatoid arthritis, with sales of $1.7 billion through the first half of 2005. And Wyeth's metabolism for making decisions has increased. Recently, when the U.S. Food and Drug Administration granted priority review status to another new drug, Tygacil, because of the antibiotic's efficacy against drug-resistant infections, Wyeth displayed its new reflexes. To keep Tygacil on a fast track, the company had to orchestrate a host of critical steps—refining the process technology, lining up supplies, ensuring quality control, allocating manufacturing capacity. The vital decisions were made one or two levels down in the biotech organization, where the expertise resided. "Instead of debating whether you can move your product into my shop, we had the decision systems in place to run it up and down the business units and move ahead rapidly with Tygacil," said Mahady. The drug was approved by the FDA in June 2005 and moved into volume production a mere three days later.

Function Versus Function

Decisions that cut across functions are some of the most important a company faces. Indeed, cross-functional collaboration has become an axiom of business, essential for arriving at the best answers for the company and its customers. But fluid decision making across functional teams remains a constant challenge, even for companies known for doing it well, like Toyota and Dell. For instance, a team that thinks it's more efficient to make a decision without consulting other functions may wind up missing out on relevant input or being overruled by another team that believes—rightly or wrongly—it should have been included in the process. Many of the most important cross-functional decisions are, by their very nature, the most difficult to orchestrate, and that can string out the process and lead to sparring between fiefdoms and costly indecision.

The theme here is a lack of clarity about who has the D. For example, at a global auto manufacturer that was missing its milestones for rolling out new models—and was paying the price in falling sales—it turned out that marketers and product developers were confused about which function was responsible for making decisions about standard features and color ranges for new models. When we asked the marketing team who had the D about which features should be standard, 83% said the marketers did. When we posed the same question to product developers, 64% said the responsibility rested with them. (See the exhibit "A Recipe for a Decision-Making Bottleneck.")

The practical difficulty of connecting functions through smooth decision making crops up frequently at retailers. John Lewis, the leading department store chain in the United Kingdom, might reasonably expect to overcome this sort of challenge more readily than other retailers. Spedan Lewis, who built the business in

---

A recipe for a decision-making bottleneck

At one automaker we studied, marketers and product developers were confused about who was responsible for making decisions about new models.

When we asked, "Who has the right to decide which features will be standard?"
64% of product developers said, "We do."
83% of marketers said, "We do."

When we asked, "Who has the right to decide which colors will be offered?"
77% of product developers said, "We do."
61% of marketers said, "We do."

Not surprisingly, the new models were delayed.

---

the early twentieth century, was a pioneer in employee ownership. A strong connection between managers and employees permeated every aspect of the store's operations and remained vital to the company as it grew into the largest employee-owned business in the United Kingdom, with 59,600 employees and more than £5 billion in revenues in 2004.

Even at John Lewis, however, with its heritage of co-operation and teamwork, cross-functional decision making can be hard to sustain. Take salt and pepper mills, for instance. John Lewis, which prides itself on having great selection, stocked nearly 50 SKUs of salt and pepper mills, while most competitors stocked around 20. The company's buyers saw an opportunity to increase sales and reduce complexity by offering a smaller number of popular and well-chosen products in each price point and style.

When John Lewis launched the new range, sales fell. This made no sense to the buyers until they visited the stores and saw how the merchandise was displayed. The buyers had made their decision without fully involving the sales staff, who therefore did not understand the strategy behind the new selection. As a result, the sellers had cut shelf space in half to match the reduction in range, rather than devoting the same amount of shelf space to stocking more of each product.

To fix the communication problem, John Lewis needed to clarify decision roles. The buyers were given the D on how much space to allocate to each product category. If the space allocation didn't make sense to the sales staff, however, they had the authority to raise their concerns and force a new round of negotiations. They also had responsibility for implementing product layouts in the stores. When the communication was sorted out and shelf space was restored, sales of the salt and pepper mills climbed well above original levels.

Crafting a decision-making process that connected the buying and selling functions for salt and pepper mills was relatively easy; rolling it out across the entire business was more challenging. Salt and pepper mills are just one of several hundred product categories for John Lewis. This element of scale is one reason why cross-functional bottlenecks are not easy to unclog. Different functions have different incentives and goals, which are often in conflict. When it comes down to a struggle between two functions, there may be good reasons to locate the D in either place—buying or selling, marketing or product development.

Here, as elsewhere, someone needs to think objectively about where value is created and assign decision roles accordingly. Eliminating cross-functional bottle-necks actually has less to do with shifting decision-making responsibilities between departments and more to do with ensuring that the people with relevant information are allowed to share it. The decision maker is important, of course, but more important is designing a system that aligns decision making and makes it routine.

Inside Versus Outside Partners

Decision making within an organization is hard enough. Trying to make decisions between separate organizations on different continents adds layers of complexity that can scuttle the best strategy. Companies that outsource capabilities in pursuit of cost and quality advantages face this very challenge. Which decisions should be made internally? Which can be delegated to outsourcing partners?

These questions are also relevant for strategic partners—a global bank working with an IT contractor on a systems development project, for example, or a media company that acquires content from a studio—and for companies conducting part of their business through franchisees. There is no right answer to who should have the power to decide what. But the wrong approach is to assume that contractual arrangements can provide the answer.

An outdoor-equipment company based in the United States discovered this recently when it decided to scale up production of gas patio heaters for the lower end of the

The Decision-Driven Organization

THE DEFINING CHARACTERISTIC OF HIGH-PERFORMING organizations is their ability to make good decisions and to make them happen quickly. The companies that succeed tend to follow a few clear principles.

Some Decisions Matter More than Others

The decisions that are crucial to building value in the business are the ones that matter most. Some of them will be the big strategic decisions, but just as important are the critical operating decisions that drive the business day to day and are vital to effective execution.

Action Is the Goal

Good decision making doesn't end with a decision; it ends with implementation. The objective shouldn't be consensus, which often becomes an obstacle to action, but buy in.

Ambiguity Is the Enemy

Clear accountability is essential: Who contributes input, who makes the decision, and who carries it out? Without clarity, gridlock and delay are the most likely outcomes. Clarity doesn't necessarily mean concentrating authority in a few people; it means defining who has responsibility to make decisions, who has input, and who is charged with putting them into action.

---

market. The company had some success manufacturing high-end products in China. But with the advent of superdiscounters like Wal-Mart, Target, and Home Depot, the company realized it needed to move more of its production overseas to feed these retailers with lower-cost offerings. The timetable left little margin for error: The company started tooling up factories in April and June of 2004, hoping to be ready for the Christmas season.

Speed and Adaptability Are Crucial

A company that makes good decisions quickly has a higher metabolism, which allows it to act on opportunities and overcome obstacles. The best decision makers create an environment where people can come together quickly and efficiently to make the most important decisions.

Decision Roles Trump the Organizational Chart

No decision-making structure will be perfect for every decision. The key is to involve the right people at the right level in the right part of the organization at the right time.

A Well-Aligned Organization Reinforces Roles

Clear decision roles are critical, but they are not enough. If an organization does not reinforce the right approach to decision making through its measures and incentives, information flows, and culture, the behavior won't become routine.

Practicing Beats Preaching

Involve the people who will live with the new decision roles in designing them. The very process of thinking about new decision behaviors motivates people to adopt them.

Right away, there were problems. Although the Chinese manufacturing partners understood costs, they had little idea what American consumers wanted. When expensive designs arrived from the head office in the United States, Chinese plant managers made compromises to meet contracted cost targets. They used a lower grade material, which discolored. They placed the power switch in a spot that was inconvenient

A Decision Diagnostic

CONSIDER THE LAST THREE MEANINGFUL decisions you've been involved in and ask yourself the following questions.

1. Were the decisions right?

2. Were they made with appropriate speed?

3. Were they executed well?

4. Were the right people involved, in the right way?

5. Was it clear for each decision

    • who would recommend a solution?

    • who would provide input?

    • who had the final say?

    • who would be responsible for following through?

6. Were the decision roles, process, and time frame respected?

7. Were the decisions based on appropriate facts?

8. To the extent that there were divergent facts or opinions, was it clear who had the D?

9. Were the decision makers at the appropriate level in the company?

10. Did the organization's measures and incentives encourage the people involved to make the right decisions?

---

for the user but easier to build. Instead of making certain parts from a single casting, they welded materials together, which looked terrible.

To fix these problems, the U.S. executives had to draw clear lines around which decisions should be made on which side of the ocean. The company broke down the design and manufacturing process into five steps and analyzed how decisions were made at each step. The company was also much more explicit about what the manufacturing specs would include and what the manufacturer was expected to do with them. The objective was not simply to clarify decision roles but to make sure those roles corresponded directly to the sources of value in the business. If a decision would affect the look and feel of the finished product, headquarters would have to sign off on it. But if a decision would not affect the customer's experience, it could be made in China. If, for example, Chinese engineers found a less expensive material that didn't compromise the product's look, feel, and functionality, they could make that change on their own.

To help with the transition to this system, the company put a team of engineers on-site in China to ensure a smooth handoff of the specs and to make decisions on issues that would become complex and time-consuming if elevated to the home office. Marketing executives in the home office insisted that it should take a customer ten minutes and no more than six steps to assemble the product at home. The company's engineers in China, along with the Chinese manufacturing team, had input into this assembly requirement and were responsible for execution. But the D resided with headquarters, and the requirement became a major design factor. Decisions about logistics, however, became the province of the engineering team in China: It would figure out how to package the heaters so that one-third more boxes would fit into a container, which reduced shipping costs substantially.

If managers suddenly realize that they're spending less time sitting through meetings wondering why they are there, that's an early signal that companies have become better at making decisions. When meetings start with a common understanding about who is responsible for providing valuable input and who has the D, an organization's decision-making metabolism will get a boost.

No single lever turns a decision-challenged organization into a decision-driven one, of course, and no blueprint can provide for all the contingencies and business shifts a company is bound to encounter. The most successful companies use simple tools that help them recognize potential bottlenecks and think through decision roles and responsibilities with each change in the business environment. That's difficult to do—and even more difficult for competitors to copy. But by taking some very practical steps, any company can become more effective, beginning with its next decision.

PAUL ROGERS is a partner with Bain & Company in London and leads Bain's global organization practice. **MARCIA BLENKO** is a partner at Bain & Company in Boston and leads Bain's North American organization practice.

Originally published in January 2006. Reprint R0601D

How (Un)ethical Are You?

by Mahzarin R. Banaji, Max H. Bazerman, and Dolly Chugh

ANSWER TRUE OR FALSE: "I am an ethical manager."

If you answered "true," here's an uncomfortable fact: You're probably not. Most of us believe that we are ethical and unbiased. We imagine we're good decision makers, able to objectively size up a job candidate or a venture deal and reach a fair and rational conclusion that's in our, and our organization's, best interests. But more than two decades of research confirms that, in reality, most of us fall woefully short of our inflated self-perception. We're deluded by what Yale psychologist David Armor calls the illusion of objectivity, the notion that we're free of the very biases we're so quick to recognize in others. What's more, these unconscious, or implicit, biases can be contrary to our consciously held, explicit beliefs. We may believe with confidence and conviction that a job candidate's race has no bearing on our hiring decisions or that we're immune to conflicts of interest. But psychological research routinely exposes counterintentional, unconscious biases. The prevalence of these biases suggests that even the most well-meaning person unwittingly allows unconscious thoughts and feelings to influence seemingly objective decisions. These flawed judgments are ethically problematic and undermine managers' fundamental work—to recruit and retain superior talent, boost the performance of individuals and teams, and collaborate effectively with partners.

This article explores four related sources of unintentional unethical decision making: implicit forms of prejudice, bias that favors one's own group, conflict of interest, and a tendency to overclaim credit. Because we are not consciously aware of these sources of bias, they often cannot be addressed by penalizing people for their bad decisions. Nor are they likely to be corrected through conventional ethics training. Rather, managers must bring a new type of vigilance to bear. To begin, this requires letting go of the notion that our conscious attitudes always represent what we think they do. It also demands that we abandon our faith in our own objectivity and our ability to be fair. In the following pages, we will offer strategies that can help managers recognize these pervasive, corrosive, unconscious biases and reduce their impact.

Implicit Prejudice: Bias That Emerges from Unconscious Beliefs

Most fair-minded people strive to judge others according to their merits, but our research shows how often

Idea in Brief

Are you an ethical manager? Most would probably say, "Of course!" The truth is, most of us are not.

Most of us believe that we're ethical and unbiased. We assume that we objectively size up job candidates or venture deals and reach fair and rational conclusions that are in our organization's best interests.

But the truth is, we harbor many unconscious—and unethical—biases that derail our decisions and undermine our work as managers. Hidden biases prevent us from recognizing high-potential workers and retaining talented managers. They stop us from collaborating effectively with partners. They erode our teams' performance.

They can also lead to costly lawsuits.

But how can we root out these biases if they're unconscious? Fortunately, as a manager, you can take deliberate actions to counteract their pull. **Regularly audit your decisions.** Have you, for example, hired a disproportionate number of people of your own race? **Expose yourself to non-stereotypical environments** that challenge your biases. If your department is led by men, spend time in one with women in leadership positions. And **consider counterintuitive options** when making decisions. Don't rely on a mental short-list of candidates for a new assignment; consider every employee with relevant qualifications.

people instead judge according to unconscious stereotypes and attitudes, or "implicit prejudice." What makes implicit prejudice so common and persistent is that it is rooted in the fundamental mechanics of thought. Early on, we learn to associate things that commonly go together and expect them to inevitably coexist: thunder and rain, for instance, or gray hair and old age. This skill—to perceive and learn from associations—often serves us well.

But, of course, our associations only reflect approximations of the truth; they are rarely applicable to every

Idea in Practice

Unconscious Biases

Are the following unconscious biases levying what amounts to a "stereotype tax" on your company?

Implicit prejudice. Judging according to unconscious stereotypes rather than merit exacts a high business cost. Exposed to images that juxtapose physical disabilities with mental weakness or portray poor people as lazy, even the most consciously unbiased person is bound to make biased associations. As a result, we routinely overlook highly qualified candidates for assignments.

In-group favoritism. Granting favors to people with your same background—your nationality or alma mater—effectively discriminates against those who are different from you. Consider the potential cost of offering bonuses to employees who refer their friends for job openings: hires who may not have made the grade *without* in-group favoritism.

Overclaiming credit. Most of us consider ourselves above average. But when every member of a team thinks he's making the biggest contribution, each starts to think the others aren't pulling their weight. That jeopardizes future collaborations. It also frustrates talented workers who may resign because they feel underappreciated.

Counteract Biases

To keep yourself from making similarly skewed calls, consider these guidelines:

encounter. Rain doesn't always accompany thunder, and the young can also go gray. Nonetheless, because we automatically make such associations to help us organize our world, we grow to trust them, and they can blind us to those instances in which the associations are not accurate—when they don't align with our expectations.

Because implicit prejudice arises from the ordinary and unconscious tendency to make associations, it is distinct from conscious forms of prejudice, such as overt racism or sexism. This distinction explains why people who are free from conscious prejudice may still

Gather better data. Expose your own implicit biases. Take the Implicit Association Test (at http://implicit.harvard.edu). If you discover gender or racial biases, examine your hiring and promotion decisions in that new light. When working with others, have team members estimate their colleagues' contributions *before* they claim their own credit.

Rid your workplace of stereotypical cues. Think about the biased associations your workplace may foster. Do your company's advertising and marketing materials frequently include sports metaphors or high-tech jargon? Make a conscious effort to curb such "insider" language—making your products more appealing to a diverse customer base.

And if your department invariably promotes the same type of manager—highly analytic, for instance—shadow a department that values a different—perhaps more conceptual—skill-set.

Broaden your mind-set when making decisions. Apply the "veil of ignorance" to your next managerial decision. Suppose you're considering a new policy that would give more vacation time to all employees but eliminate the flextime that has allowed new parents to keep working. How would your opinion differ if you were a parent or childless? Male or female? Healthy or unhealthy? You'll learn how strongly implicit biases influence you.

harbor biases and act accordingly. Exposed to images that juxtapose black men and violence, portray women as sex objects, imply that the physically disabled are mentally weak and the poor are lazy, even the most consciously unbiased person is bound to make biased associations. These associations play out in the workplace just as they do anywhere else.

In the mid-1990s, Tony Greenwald, a professor of psychology at the University of Washington, developed an experimental tool called the Implicit Association Test (IAT) to study unconscious bias. A computerized version

Are You Biased?

ARE YOU WILLING TO BET that you feel the same way toward European-Americans as you do toward African-Americans? How about women versus men? Or older people versus younger ones? Think twice before you take that bet. Visit implicit.harvard.edu or www.tolerance.org/hidden_bias to examine your unconscious attitudes.

The Implicit Association Tests available on these sites reveal unconscious beliefs by asking takers to make split-second associations between words with positive or negative connotations and images representing different types of people. The various tests on these sites expose the differences—or the alignment—between test takers' conscious and unconscious attitudes toward people of different races, sexual orientation, or physical characteristics. Data gathered from over 2.5 million online tests and further research tells us that unconscious biases are:

- **widely prevalent.** At least 75% of test takers show an implicit bias favoring the young, the rich, and whites.

- **robust.** The mere conscious desire not to be biased does not eliminate implicit bias.

---

of the test requires subjects to rapidly classify words and images as "good" or "bad." Using a keyboard, test takers must make split-second "good/bad" distinctions between words like "love," "joy," "pain," and "sorrow" and at the same time sort images of faces that are (depending on the bias in question) black or white, young or old, fat or thin, and so on. The test exposes implicit biases by detecting subtle shifts in reaction time that can occur when test takers are required to pair different sets of words and faces. Subjects who consciously believe that

- **contrary to conscious intention.** Although people tend to report little or no *conscious* bias against African-Americans, Arabs, Arab-Americans, Jews, gay men, lesbians, or the poor, they show substantial biases on implicit measures.

- **different in degree depending on group status.** Minority group members tend to show less implicit preference for their own group than majority group members show for theirs. For example, African-Americans report strong preference for their group on explicit measures but show relatively less implicit preference in the tests. Conversely, white Americans report a low explicit bias for their group but a higher implicit bias.

- **consequential.** Those who show higher levels of bias on the IAT are also likely to behave in ways that are more biased in face-to-face interactions with members of the group they are biased against and in the choices they make, such as hiring decisions.

- **costly.** Research currently under way in our lab suggests that implicit bias generates a "stereotype tax"—negotiators leave money on the table because biases cause them to miss opportunities to learn about their opponent and thus create additional value through mutually beneficial trade-offs.

they have no negative feelings toward, say, black Americans or the elderly are nevertheless likely to be slower to associate elderly or black faces with the "good" words than they are to associate youthful or white faces with "good" words.

Since 1998, when Greenwald, Brian Nosek, and Mahzarin Banaji put the IAT online, people from around the world have taken over 2.5 million tests, confirming and extending the findings of more traditional laboratory experiments. Both show implicit biases to be strong and pervasive. (For more information on the IAT, see the sidebar "Are You Biased?").

Biases are also likely to be costly. In controlled experiments, psychologists Laurie Rudman at Rutgers and Peter Glick at Lawrence University have studied how implicit biases may work to exclude qualified people from certain roles. One set of experiments examined the relationship between participants' implicit gender stereotypes and their hiring decisions. Those holding stronger implicit biases were less likely to select a qualified woman who exhibited stereotypically "masculine" personality qualities, such as ambition or independence, for a job requiring stereotypically "feminine" qualities, such as interpersonal skills. Yet they would select a qualified man exhibiting these same qualities. The hirers' biased perception was that the woman was less likely to be socially skilled than the man, though their qualifications were in fact the same. These results suggest that implicit biases may exact costs by subtly excluding qualified people from the very organizations that seek their talents.

Legal cases also reveal the real costs of implicit biases, both economic and social. Consider *Price Waterhouse v. Hopkins*. Despite logging more billable hours than her peers, bringing in $25 million to the company, and earning the praise of her clients, Ann Hopkins was turned down for partner, and she sued. The details of the case reveal that her evaluators were explicitly prejudiced in their attitudes. For example, they had commented that Ann "overcompensated for being a woman" and needed a "course at charm school." But perhaps more damning from a legal standpoint was blunt testimony from experimental research. Testifying as an expert witness for the defense, psychology professor Susan Fiske, now at Princeton University, argued that the potential for biased decision making is *inherent* in a system in which a person has "solo" status—that is, a system in which the person is the only one of a kind (the only woman, the only African-American, the only person with a disability, and the like). Judge Gerhard Gesell concluded that "a far more subtle process [than the usual discriminatory intent] is involved" in the assessments made of Ann Hopkins, and she won both in a lower court and in the Supreme Court in what is now a landmark case in discrimination law.

Likewise, the 1999 case of *Thomas v. Kodak* demonstrates that implicit biases can be the basis for rulings. Here, the court posed the question of "whether the employer consciously intended to base the evaluations on race or simply did so because of unthinking stereotypes or bias." The court concluded that plaintiffs can indeed challenge "subjective evaluations which could easily mask covert or unconscious race discrimination." Although courts are careful not to assign responsibility easily for unintentional biases, these cases demonstrate the potential for corporate liability that such patterns of behavior could unwittingly create.

In-Group Favoritism: Bias That Favors Your Group

Think about some of the favors you have done in recent years, whether for a friend, a relative, or a colleague.

Have you helped someone get a useful introduction, admission to a school, or a job? Most of us are glad to help out with such favors. Not surprisingly, we tend to do more favors for those we know, and those we know tend to be like ourselves: people who share our nationality, social class, and perhaps religion, race, employer, or alma mater. This all sounds rather innocent. What's wrong with asking your neighbor, the university dean, to meet with a coworker's son? Isn't it just being helpful to recommend a former sorority sister for a job or to talk to your banker cousin when a friend from church gets turned down for a home loan?

Few people set out to exclude anyone through such acts of kindness. But when those in the majority or those in power allocate scarce resources (such as jobs, promotions, and mortgages) to people just like them, they effectively discriminate against those who are different from them. Such "in-group favoritism" amounts to giving extra credit for group membership. Yet while discriminating against those who are different is considered unethical, helping people close to us is often viewed favorably. Think about the number of companies that explicitly encourage this by offering hiring bonuses to employees who refer their friends for job opportunities.

But consider the finding that banks in the United States are more likely to deny a mortgage application from a black person than from a white person, even when the applicants are equally qualified. The common view has been that banks are hostile to African-Americans. While this may be true of some banks and some loan officers, social psychologist David Messick has argued that in-group favoritism is more likely to be at the root of such discriminatory lending. A white loan officer may feel hopeful or lenient toward an unqualified white applicant while following the bank's lending standards strictly with an unqualified black applicant. In denying the black applicant's mortgage, the loan officer may not be expressing hostility toward blacks so much as favoritism toward whites. It's a subtle but crucial distinction.

The ethical cost is clear and should be reason enough to address the problem. But such inadvertent bias produces an additional effect: It erodes the bottom line. Lenders who discriminate in this way, for example, incur bad-debt costs they could have avoided if their lending decisions were more objective. They also may find themselves exposed to damaging publicity or discrimination lawsuits if the skewed lending pattern is publicly revealed. In a different context, companies may pay a real cost for marginal hires who wouldn't have made the grade but for the sympathetic hiring manager swayed by in-group favoritism.

In-group favoritism is tenacious when membership confers clear advantages, as it does, for instance, among whites and other dominant social groups. (It may be weaker or absent among people whose group membership offers little societal advantage.) Thus for a wide array of managerial tasks—from hiring, firing, and promoting to contracting services and forming partnerships—qualified minority candidates are subtly and unconsciously discriminated against, sometimes simply because they are in the minority: There are not enough of them to counter the propensity for in-group favoritism in the majority.

Overclaiming Credit: Bias That Favors You

It's only natural for successful people to hold positive views about themselves. But many studies show that the majority of people consider themselves above average on a host of measures, from intelligence to driving ability. Business executives are no exception. We tend to overrate our individual contribution to groups, which, bluntly put, tends to lead to an overblown sense of entitlement. We become the unabashed, repeated beneficiaries of this unconscious bias, and the more we think only of our own contributions, the less fairly we judge others with whom we work.

Lab research demonstrates this most personal of biases. At Harvard, Eugene Caruso, Nick Epley, and Max Bazerman recently asked MBA students in study groups to estimate what portion of their group's work each had done. The sum of the contribution by all members, of course, must add up to 100%. But the researchers found that the totals for each study group averaged 139%. In a related study, Caruso and his colleagues uncovered rampant overestimates by academic authors of their contribution to shared research projects. Sadly, but not surprisingly, the more the sum of the total estimated group effort exceeded 100% (in other words, the more credit each person claimed), the less the parties wanted to collaborate in the future.

Likewise in business, claiming too much credit can destabilize alliances. When each party in a strategic partnership claims too much credit for its own contribution and becomes skeptical about whether the other is doing its fair share, they both tend to reduce their contributions to compensate. This has obvious repercussions for the joint venture's performance.

Unconscious overclaiming can be expected to reduce the performance and longevity of groups within organizations, just as it diminished the academic authors' willingness to collaborate. It can also take a toll on employee commitment. Think about how employees perceive raises. Most are not so different from the children at Lake Wobegon, believing that they, too, rank in the upper half of their peer group. But many necessarily get pay increases that are below the average. If an employee learns of a colleague's greater compensation—while honestly believing that he himself is more deserving—resentment may be natural. At best, his resentment might translate into reduced commitment and performance. At worst, he may leave the organization that, it seems, doesn't appreciate his contribution.

Conflict of Interest: Bias That Favors Those Who Can Benefit You

Everyone knows that conflict of interest can lead to intentionally corrupt behavior. But numerous psychological experiments show how powerfully such conflicts can unintentionally skew decision making. (For an examination of the evidence in one business arena, see Max Bazerman,

George Loewenstein, and Don Moore's November 2002 HBR article, "Why Good Accountants Do Bad Audits.") These experiments suggest that the work world is rife with situations in which such conflicts lead honest, ethical professionals to unconsciously make unsound and unethical recommendations.

Physicians, for instance, face conflicts of interest when they accept payment for referring patients into clinical trials. While, surely, most physicians consciously believe that their referrals are the patient's best clinical option, how do they know that the promise of payment did not skew their decisions? Similarly, many lawyers earn fees based on their clients' awards or settlements. Since going to trial is expensive and uncertain, settling out of court is often an attractive option for the lawyer. Attorneys may consciously believe that settling is in their clients' best interests. But how can they be objective, unbiased judges under these circumstances?

Research done with brokerage house analysts demonstrates how conflict of interest can unconsciously distort decision making. A survey of analysts conducted by the financial research service First Call showed that during a period in 2000 when the Nasdaq dropped 60%, fully 99% of brokerage analysts' client recommendations remained "strong buy," "buy," or "hold." What accounts for this discrepancy between what was happening and what was recommended? The answer may lie in a system that fosters conflicts of interest. A portion of analysts' pay is based on brokerage firm revenues. Some firms even tie analysts' compensation to the amount of business the analysts bring in from clients, giving analysts an obvious incentive to prolong and extend their relationships with clients. But to assume that during this Nasdaq free fall all brokerage house analysts were consciously corrupt, milking their clients to exploit this incentive system, defies common sense. Surely there were some bad apples. But how much more likely it is that most of these analysts believed their recommendations were sound and in their clients' best interests. What many didn't appreciate was that the built-in conflict of interest in their compensation incentives made it impossible for them to see the implicit bias in their own flawed recommendations.

Trying Harder Isn't Enough

As companies keep collapsing into financial scandal and ruin, corporations are responding with ethics-training programs for managers, and many of the world's leading business schools have created new courses and chaired professorships in ethics. Many of these efforts focus on teaching broad principles of moral philosophy to help managers understand the ethical challenges they face.

We applaud these efforts, but we doubt that a well-intentioned, just-try-harder approach will fundamentally improve the quality of executives' decision making. To do that, ethics training must be broadened to include what is now known about how our minds work and must expose managers directly to the unconscious mechanisms that underlie biased decision making. And it must provide managers with exercises and interventions that can root out the biases that lead to bad decisions.

Managers can make wiser, more ethical decisions if they become mindful of their unconscious biases. But how can we get at something outside our conscious awareness? By bringing the conscious mind to bear. Just as the driver of a misaligned car deliberately counteracts its pull, so can managers develop conscious strategies to counteract the pull of their unconscious biases. What's required is vigilance—continual awareness of the forces that can cause decision making to veer from its intended course and continual adjustments to counteract them. Those adjustments fall into three general categories: collecting data, shaping the environment, and broadening the decision-making process.

Collect Data

The first step to reducing unconscious bias is to collect data to reveal its presence. Often, the data will be counterintuitive. Consider many people's surprise to learn of their own gender and racial biases on the IAT. Why the surprise? Because most of us trust the "statistics" our intuition provides. Better data are easily, but rarely, collected. One way to get those data is to examine our decisions in a systematic way.

Remember the MBA study groups whose participants overestimated their individual contributions to the group effort so that the totals averaged 139%? When the researchers asked group members to estimate what each of the other members' contributions were *before* claiming their own, the total fell to 121%. The tendency to claim too much credit still persisted, but this strategy of "unpacking" the work reduced the magnitude of the bias. In environments characterized by "I deserve more than you're giving me" claims, merely asking team members to unpack the contributions of others before claiming their own share of the pot usually aligns claims more closely with what's actually deserved. As this example demonstrates, such systematic audits of both individual and group decision-making processes can occur even as the decisions are being made.

Unpacking is a simple strategy that managers should routinely use to evaluate the fairness of their own claims within the organization. But they can also apply it in any situation where team members or subordinates may be overclaiming. For example, in explaining a raise that an employee feels is inadequate, a manager should ask the subordinate not what he thinks he alone deserves but what he considers an appropriate raise after taking into account each coworker's contribution and the pool available for pay increases. Similarly, when an individual feels she's doing more than her fair share of a team's work, asking her to consider other people's efforts before estimating her own can help align her perception with reality, restore her commitment, and reduce a skewed sense of entitlement.

Taking the IAT is another valuable strategy for collecting data. We recommend that you and others in your organization use the test to expose your own implicit biases. But one word of warning: Because the test is an educational and research tool, not a selection or evaluation tool, it is critical that you consider your results and others' to be private information. Simply knowing the magnitude and pervasiveness of your own biases can help direct your attention to areas of decision making that are in need of careful examination and reconsideration. For example, a manager whose testing reveals a bias toward certain groups ought to examine her hiring practices to see if she has indeed been disproportionately favoring those groups. But because so many people harbor such biases, they can also be generally acknowledged, and that knowledge can be used as the basis for changing the way decisions are made. It is important to guard against using pervasiveness to justify complacency and inaction: Pervasiveness of bias is not a mark of its appropriateness any more than poor eyesight is considered so ordinary a condition that it does not require corrective lenses.

Shape Your Environment

Research shows that implicit attitudes can be shaped by external cues in the environment. For example, Curtis Hardin and colleagues at UCLA used the IAT to study whether subjects' implicit race bias would be affected if the test was administered by a black investigator. One group of students took the test under the guidance of a white experimenter; another group took the test with a black experimenter. The mere presence of a black experimenter, Hardin found, reduced the level of subjects' implicit antiblack bias on the IAT. Numerous similar studies have shown similar effects with other social groups. What accounts for such shifts? We can speculate that experimenters in classrooms are assumed to be competent, in charge, and authoritative. Subjects guided by a black experimenter attribute these positive characteristics to that person, and then perhaps to the group as a whole. These findings suggest that one remedy for implicit bias is to expose oneself to images and social environments that challenge stereotypes.

We know of a judge whose court is located in a predominantly African-American neighborhood. Because of the crime and arrest patterns in the community, most people the judge sentences are black. The judge confronted a paradox. On the one hand, she took a judicial oath to be objective and egalitarian, and indeed she consciously believed that her decisions were unbiased. On the other hand, every day she was exposed to an environment that reinforced the association between black men and crime. Although she consciously rejected racial stereotypes, she suspected that she harbored unconscious prejudices merely from working in a segregated world. Immersed in this environment each day, she wondered if it was possible to give the defendants a fair hearing.

Rather than allow her environment to reinforce a bias, the judge created an alternative environment. She spent a vacation week sitting in a fellow judge's court in a neighborhood where the criminals being tried were predominantly white. Case after case challenged the stereotype of blacks as criminal and whites as law abiding and so challenged any bias against blacks that she might have harbored.

Think about the possibly biased associations your workplace fosters. Is there, perhaps, a "wall of fame" with pictures of high achievers all cast from the same mold? Are certain types of managers invariably promoted? Do people overuse certain analogies drawn from stereotypical or narrow domains of knowledge (sports metaphors, for instance, or cooking terms)? Managers can audit their organization to uncover such patterns or cues that unwittingly lead to stereotypical associations.

If an audit reveals that the environment may be promoting unconscious biased or unethical behavior, consider creating countervailing experiences, as the judge did. For example, if your department reinforces the stereotype of men as naturally dominant in a hierarchy (most managers are male, and most assistants are female), find a department with women in leadership positions and set up a shadow program. Both groups will benefit from the exchange of best practices, and your group will be quietly exposed to counterstereotypical cues. Managers sending people out to spend time in clients' organizations as a way to improve service should take care to select organizations likely to counter stereotypes reinforced in your own company.

Broaden Your Decision Making

Imagine that you are making a decision in a meeting about an important company policy that will benefit some groups of employees more than others. A policy might, for example, provide extra vacation time for all employees but eliminate the flex time that has allowed many new parents to balance work with their family responsibilities. Another policy might lower the mandatory retirement age, eliminating some older workers but creating advancement opportunities for younger ones. Now pretend that, as you make your decisions, you don't know which group you belong to. That is, you don't know whether you are senior or junior, married or single, gay or straight, a parent or childless, male or female, healthy or unhealthy. You will eventually find out, but not until after the decision has been made. In this hypothetical scenario, what decision would you make? Would you be willing to risk being in the group disadvantaged by your own decision? How would your decisions differ if you could make them wearing various identities not your own?

This thought experiment is a version of philosopher John Rawls's concept of the "veil of ignorance," which posits that only a person ignorant of his own identity is capable of a truly ethical decision. Few of us can assume the veil completely, which is precisely why hidden biases, even when identified, are so difficult to correct. Still, applying the veil of ignorance to your next important managerial decision may offer some insight into how strongly implicit biases influence you.

Just as managers can expose bias by collecting data before acting on intuition, they can take other preemptive steps. What list of names do you start with when considering whom to send to a training program, recommend for a new assignment, or nominate for a fast-track position? Most of us can quickly and with little concentration come up with such a list. But keep in mind that your intuition is prone to implicit prejudice (which will strongly favor dominant and well-liked groups), in-group favoritism (which will favor people in your own group), overclaiming (which will favor you), and conflict of interest (which will favor people whose interests affect your own). Instead of relying on a mental short list when making personnel decisions, start with a full list of names of employees who have relevant qualifications.

Using a broad list of names has several advantages. The most obvious is that talent may surface that might otherwise be overlooked. Less obvious but equally important, the very act of considering a counterstereotypical choice at the conscious level can reduce implicit bias. In fact, merely thinking about hypothetical, counterstereotypical scenarios—such as what it would be like to trust a complex presentation to a female colleague or to receive a promotion from an African-American boss—can prompt less-biased and more ethical decision making. Similarly, consciously considering counterintuitive options in the face of conflicts of interest, or when there's an opportunity to overclaim, can promote more objective and ethical decisions.

The Vigilant Manager

If you answered "true" to the question at the start of this article, you felt with some confidence that you are an ethical decision maker. How would you answer it now? It's clear that neither simple conviction nor sincere intention is enough to ensure that you are the ethical practitioner you imagine yourself to be. Managers who aspire to be ethical must challenge the assumption that they're always unbiased and acknowledge that vigilance, even more than good intention, is a defining characteristic of an ethical manager. They must actively collect data, shape their environments, and broaden their decision making. What's more, an obvious redress is available. Managers should seek every opportunity to implement affirmative action policies—not because of past wrongs done to one group or another but because of the everyday wrongs that we can now document are inherent in the ordinary, everyday behavior of good, well-intentioned people. Ironically, only those who understand their own potential for unethical behavior can become the ethical decision makers that they aspire to be.

MAHZARIN R. BANAJI is the Richard Clarke Cabot Professor of Social Ethics at Harvard University. **MAX H. BAZERMAN** is the Jesse Isidor Straus Professor of Business Administration at Harvard Business School. **DOLLY CHUGH** is a doctoral candidate in Harvard University's joint program in organizational behavior and social psychology.

Originally published in December 2003. Reprint R0312D

Make Better Decisions

by Thomas H. Davenport

IN RECENT YEARS DECISION MAKERS in both the public and private sectors have made an astounding number of poor calls. For example, the decisions to invade Iraq, not to comply with global warming treaties, to ignore Darfur, are all likely to be recorded as injudicious in history books. And how about the decisions to invest in and securitize subprime mortgage loans, or to hedge risk with credit default swaps? Those were spread across a number of companies, but single organizations, too, made bad decisions. Tenneco, once a large conglomerate, chose poorly when buying businesses and now consists of only one auto parts business. General Motors made terrible decisions about which cars to bring to market. Time Warner erred in buying AOL, and Yahoo in deciding not to sell itself to Microsoft.

Why this decision-making disorder? First, because decisions have generally been viewed as the prerogative of individuals—usually senior executives. The process employed, the information used, the logic relied on, have been left up to them, in something of a black box. Information goes in, decisions come out—and who knows what happens in between? Second, unlike other business processes, decision making has rarely been the focus of systematic analysis inside the firm. Very few organizations have "reengineered" their decisions. Yet there are just as many opportunities to improve decision making as to improve any other process.

Useful insights have been available for a long time. For example, academics defined "groupthink," the forced manufacture of consent, more than half a century ago—yet it still bedevils decision makers from the White House to company boardrooms. In the sixteenth century the Catholic Church established the devil's advocate to criticize canonization decisions—yet few organizations today formalize the advocacy of decision alternatives. Recent popular business books address a host of decision-making alternatives (see "Selected Reading").

However, although businesspeople are clearly buying and reading these books, few companies have actually adopted their recommendations. The consequences of this inattention are becoming ever more severe. It is time to take decision making out of the realm of the purely individual and idiosyncratic; organizations must help their managers employ better decision-making processes. Better processes won't guarantee better decisions, of course, but they can make them more likely.

Idea in Brief

Traditionally, decision making in organizations has rarely been the focus of systematic analysis. That may account for the astounding number of recent poor calls, such as decisions to invest in and securitize subprime mortgage loans or to hedge risk with credit default swaps. Business books are rich with insights about the decision process, but organizations have been slow to adopt their recommendations. It's time to focus on decision making, Davenport says, and he proposes four steps: (1) List and prioritize the decisions that must be made; (2) assess the factors that go into each, such as who plays what role, how often the decision must be made, and what information is available to support it; (3) design the roles, processes, systems, and behaviors your organization needs; and (4) institutionalize decision tools and assistance. The Educational Testing Service and The Stanley Works, among others, have succeeded in improving their decisions. ETS established a centralized deliberative body to make evidence-based decisions about new-product offerings, and Stanley has a Pricing Center of Excellence with internal consultants dedicated to its various business units. Leaders should bring multiple perspectives to their decision making, beware of analytical models that managers don't understand, be clear about their assumptions, practice "model management," and—because only people can revise decision criteria over time—cultivate human backups.

A Framework for Improving Decisions

Focusing on decisions doesn't necessarily require a strict focus on the mental processes of managers. (Though, admittedly, the black box deserves some unpacking.) It can mean examining the accessible components of decision making—which decisions need to be made, what information is supplied, key roles in the process, and so forth. Smart organizations make multifaceted interventions—addressing technology, information,

Selected Reading

Blink
by Malcolm Gladwell, is a paean to intuitive decision making.

The Wisdom of Crowds
by James Surowiecki, argues for large-group participation in decisions.

How We Decide
by Jonah Lehrer, addresses the psychobiology of decision making and the limits of rationality.

Predictably Irrational
by Dan Ariely, considers behavioral economics and its implications for decision making.

Nudge
by Richard Thaler and Cass Sunstein, is influencing discussions about behavior-oriented policy in Washington, DC.

Two books on analytical and automated decision making:

Competing on Analytics
by Thomas H. Davenport and Jeanne G. Harris.

Super Crunchers
by Ian Ayres.

---

organizational structure, methods, and personnel. They can improve decision making in four steps:

1. Identification
Managers should begin by listing the decisions that must be made and deciding which are most important—for example, "the top 10 decisions required to execute our strategy" or "the top 10 decisions that have to go well if we are to meet our financial goals." Some decisions

will be rare and highly strategic ("What acquisitions will allow us to gain the necessary market share?") while others will be frequent and on the front lines ("How should we decide how much to pay on claims?"). Without some prioritization, all decisions will be treated as equal—which probably means that the important ones won't be analyzed with sufficient care.

2. Inventory

In addition to identifying key decisions, you should assess the factors that go into each of them. Who plays what role in the decision? How often does it occur? What information is available to support it? How well is the decision typically made? Such an examination helps an organization understand which decisions need improvement and what processes might make them more effective, while establishing a common language for discussing decision making.

3. Intervention

Having narrowed down your list of decisions and examined what's involved in making each, you can design the roles, processes, systems, and behaviors your organization should be using to make them. The key to effective decision interventions is a broad, inclusive approach that considers all methods of improvement and addresses all aspects of the decision process—including execution of the decision, which is often overlooked.

4. Institutionalization

Organizations need to give managers the tools and assistance to "decide how to decide" on an ongoing basis.

At Air Products and Chemicals, for example, managers are trained to determine whether a particular decision should be made unilaterally by one manager, unilaterally after consultation with a group, by a group through a majority vote, or by group consensus. In addition, they determine who will be responsible for making the decision, who will be held accountable for results, and who needs to be consulted or informed.

Companies that are serious about institutionalizing better decision making often enlist decision experts to work with executives on improving the process. Chevron, for example, has a decision-analysis group whose members facilitate decision-framing workshops; coordinate data gathering for analysis; build and refine economic and analytical models; help project managers and decision makers interpret analyses; point out when additional information and analysis would improve a decision; conduct an assessment of decision quality; and coach decision makers. The group has trained more than 2,500 decision makers in two-day workshops and has certified 10,000 through an online training module. At Chevron all major capital projects (which are common at large oil companies) have the benefit of systematic decision analysis.

An organization that has adopted these four steps should also assess the quality of decisions after the fact. The assessment should address not only actual business results—which can involve both politics and luck—but also the decision-making process and whatever information the manager relied on. Chevron regularly performs "lookbacks" on major decisions, and assesses not only outcomes but also how the decision might have employed a better process or addressed uncertainty better.

Let's look at how two companies have improved their decision making.

Better New-Product Decisions at ETS

The Educational Testing Service develops and administers such widely recognized tests as the SAT, the GRE, the TOEFL, and the AP. In 2007 Kurt Landgraf, ETS's CEO, concluded that the organization needed to accelerate and improve decisions about new products and services if it was to continue competing effectively. ETS had previously employed a stage-gate approval process for new offerings, but the organization's matrixed structure and diffuse decision-making responsibility made the process ineffective.

Landgraf asked T.J. Elliott, ETS's vice president of strategic workforce solutions, and Marisa Farnum, the associate vice president for technology transfer, to lead a team that would examine the decision process. The team found several fundamental problems. First, decision makers often lacked information about the intellectual property, partners, cycle times, and likely market for new offerings. Second, it was unclear who played what roles when a decision was being made. Third, the structure of the process was vague.

Elliott and Farnum's team created a new process intended to lead to more evidence-based decisions. It introduced a centralized deliberative body to make decisions about new offerings, developed forms that required new metrics for and information about each proposal, and established standards for what constituted strong evidence that the offering fit with ETS strategy and likely market demand. The process has been in operation for 20 months and is widely regarded as a major improvement. It has clearly resulted in fewer bad product-launch decisions. However, the deliberative body has realized that proposals must be nurtured from an earlier stage to create more good offerings. The scope of its governance was expanded recently to evaluate and prioritize all product-adaptation and new-product opportunities.

Better Pricing Decisions at The Stanley Works

The Stanley Works, a maker of tools and other products for construction, industry, and security, has been operating its Pricing Center of Excellence since 2003. Under the banner of the Stanley Fulfillment System, a broad initiative for continual improvement in operations, Stanley had identified several decision domains that were critical to its success, including pricing, sales and operational planning, fulfillment processes, and lean manufacturing. Because all of them had a strong information component, a center of excellence was formed for each. The pricing center brings deep knowledge of pricing, data and analysis tools, and relationships with pricing experts at consulting and software firms to Stanley's business units. It is staffed by a director, internal consultants dedicated to the business units, and IT and data-mining specialists.

The center has made a variety of interventions in how the business units reach and execute pricing decisions. Over time it has developed several pricing methodologies and is now focusing on pricing optimization approaches. It has recommended assigning pricing responsibilities to the business unit managers. It holds regular "gross margin calls" with the units to share successes and review failures. (Stanley's CEO, John Lundgren, and its COO, Jim Loree, frequently participate.) Pricing outcomes have been added to personnel evaluations and compensation reviews. An offshore supplier has been engaged to gather and analyze competitors' prices. The center has helped to develop automated decision making, such as a process for authorizing promotional events. It uses "white space analysis" to analyze customer sales data and identify opportunities for additional sales or margin. It also trains the business units on pricing methods, participates in project start-ups, does coaching and mentoring, and disseminates innovations and best practices in pricing.

The results of the center's work speak for themselves: Gross margin at Stanley grew from 33.9% to more than 40% in six years. The changes have delivered more than $200 million in incremental value to the firm. Bert Davis, Stanley's head of business transformation and information systems, says, "We tried to improve pricing decisions with data and analysis tools alone, but it didn't work. It was only when we established the center that we began to see real improvement in pricing decisions."

Multiple Perspectives Yield Better Results

Analytics and decision automation are among the most powerful tools for improving decision making. A growing number of firms are embracing the former both strategically and tactically, building competitive strategies around their analytical capabilities and making decisions on the basis of data and analytics. (See my article "Competing on Analytics," HBR January 2006.) Analytics are even more effective when they have been embedded in automated systems, which can make many decisions virtually in real time. (Few mortgages or insurance policies in the United States are drawn up without decision automation.)

But if one of these approaches goes awry, it can do serious damage to your business. If you're making poor decisions on loans or insurance policies with an automated system, for example, you can lose money in a torrent—just ask those bankers who issued so many low-quality subprime loans. Therefore, it's critical to balance and augment these decision tools with human intuition and judgment. Organizations should:

- Warn managers not to build into their businesses analytical models they don't understand. This means, of course, that to be effective, managers must increasingly be numerate with analytics. As the Yale economist Robert Shiller told the *McKinsey Quarterly* in April 2009, "You have to be a quantitative person if you're managing a company. The quantitative details really matter."

- Make assumptions clear. Every model has assumptions behind it, such as "Housing prices will continue to rise for the foreseeable future" or "Loan charge-off levels will remain similar to those of the past 10 years." (Both these assumptions, of course, have recently been discredited.) Knowing what the assumptions are makes it possible to anticipate when models are no longer a guide to effective decisions.

- Practice "model management," which keeps track of the models being used within an organization and monitors how well they are working to analyze and predict selected variables. Capital One, an early adopter, has many analytical models in place to support marketing and operations.

- Cultivate human backups. Automated decision systems are often used to replace human decision makers—but you lose those people at your peril. It takes an expert human being to revise decision criteria over time or know when an automated algorithm no longer works well.

It's also important to know when a particular decision approach doesn't apply. For example, analytics isn't a good fit in situations when you have to make a really fast decision. And almost all quantitative models—even predictive ones—are based on past data, so if your experience or intuition tells you that the past is no longer a good guide to the present and future, you'll

The new landscape of decision making

Ancient approaches to decision making have recently been augmented by improvements in technology and new research. But every approach has both benefits and drawbacks.

	Small-group process	Analytics	Automation	Neuroscience
	making effective decisions with just a few people	using data and quantitative analysis to support decision making	using decision rules and algorithms to automate decision processes	learning from brain research that illuminates decision making
Benefits	premature convergence on a decisions is unlikely	decisions are more likely to be correct	speed and accuracy	decision makers know when to use the emotional brain
	clear responsibilities can be assigned	the scientific method adds rigor	criteria for decisions are clear	trains the rational brain to perform more effectively
	multiple alternatives can be examined			individual decision making may be overvalued
Cautionary messages	norms for debate must be rational, not emotional	gathering enough data may be difficult and time-consuming	difficult to develop	the brain is still poorly understood
	everyone must get on board with the decision after debate	correct assumptions are crucial	decision criteria may change	

	Behavioral economics	Intuition	Wisdom of crowds
Benefits	incorporating research on economic behavior and thinking into decisions	relying on one's gut and experience to make decisions	using surveys or markets to allow decisions or inputs by large groups
	illuminates and areas of irrationality	biases easy and requires no data	those close to the issue are well positioned to know the truth
Cautionary messages	can nudge decisions in a particular direction	the subconscious can be effective at weighing options	crowd-based decisions can be very accurate
	findings in the field are still sketchy	typically the least accurate of decision approaches	members of the crowd must not influence one another
	context and wording can be used to manipulate decisions	decision makers are easily swayed by context	ongoing participation is difficult to maintain

want to employ other decision tools, or at least to create some new data and analyses. (For a quick look at the strengths and weaknesses of various approaches, see the exhibit "The New Landscape of Decision Making.")

Decisions, like any other business activity, won't get better without systematic review. If you don't know which of your decisions are most important, you won't be able to prioritize improvements. If you don't know how decisions are made in your company, you can't change the process for making them. If you don't assess the results of your changes, you're unlikely to achieve better decisions. The way to begin is simply to give decisions the attention they deserve. Without it, any success your organization achieves in decision making will be largely a matter of luck.

THOMAS H. DAVENPORT is the President's Distinguished Professor of Information Technology and Management at Babson College in Massachusetts.

Originally published in November 2009. Reprint R0911L

Why Good Leaders Make Bad Decisions

by Andrew Campbell, Jo Whitehead, and Sydney Finkelstein

DECISION MAKING LIES AT THE heart of our personal and professional lives. Every day we make decisions. Some are small, domestic, and innocuous. Others are more important, affecting people's lives, livelihoods, and well-being. Inevitably, we make mistakes along the way. The daunting reality is that enormously important decisions made by intelligent, responsible people with the best information and intentions are sometimes hopelessly flawed.

Consider Jürgen Schrempp, CEO of Daimler-Benz. He led the merger of Chrysler and Daimler against internal opposition. Nine years later, Daimler was forced to virtually give Chrysler away in a private equity deal. Steve Russell, chief executive of Boots, the UK drugstore chain, launched a health care strategy designed to differentiate the stores from competitors and grow through new health care services such as dentistry. It turned out, though, that Boots managers did not have the skills needed to succeed in health care services, and many of these markets offered little profit potential. The strategy contributed to Russell's early departure from the top job. Brigadier General Matthew Broderick, chief of the Homeland Security Operations Center, who was responsible for alerting President Bush and other senior government officials if Hurricane Katrina breached the levees in New Orleans, went home on Monday, August 29, 2005, after reporting that they seemed to be holding, despite multiple reports of breaches.

All these executives were highly qualified for their jobs, and yet they made decisions that soon seemed clearly wrong. Why? And more important, how can we avoid making similar mistakes? This is the topic we've been exploring for the past four years, and the journey has taken us deep into a field called decision neuroscience. We began by assembling a database of 83 decisions that we felt were flawed at the time they were made. From our analysis of these cases, we concluded that flawed decisions start with errors of judgment made by influential individuals. Hence we needed to understand how these errors of judgment occur.

In the following pages, we will describe the conditions that promote errors of judgment and explore ways organizations can build protections into the decision-making process to reduce the risk of mistakes. We'll conclude by showing how two leading companies applied the approach we describe. To put all this in context,

Idea in Brief

- Leaders make decisions largely through unconscious processes that neuroscientists call pattern recognition and emotional tagging. These processes usually make for quick, effective decisions, but they can be distorted by self- interest, emotional attachments, or misleading memories.

- Managers need to find systematic ways to recognize the sources of bias—what the authors call "red flag conditions"—and then design safeguards that introduce more analysis, greater debate, or stronger governance.

- By using the approach described in this article, companies will avoid many flawed decisions that are caused by the way our brains operate.

however, we first need to understand just how the human brain forms its judgments.

How the Brain Trips Up

We depend primarily on two hardwired processes for decision making. Our brains assess what's going on using pattern recognition, and we react to that information—or ignore it—because of emotional tags that are stored in our memories. Both of these processes are normally reliable; they are part of our evolutionary advantage. But in certain circumstances, both can let us down.

Pattern recognition is a complex process that integrates information from as many as 30 different parts of the brain. Faced with a new situation, we make assumptions based on prior experiences and judgments. Thus a chess master can assess a chess game and choose a

Idea in Practice

Leaders make quick decisions by recognizing patterns in the situations they encounter, bolstered by emotional associations attached to those patterns. Most of the time, the process works well, but it can result in serious mistakes when judgments are biased.

Example: When Wang Laboratories launched its own personal computer, founder An Wang chose to create a proprietary operating system even though the IBM PC was clearly becoming the standard. This blunder was influenced by his belief that IBM had cheated him early in his career, which made him reluctant to consider using a system linked to an IBM product.

To guard against distorted decision making and strengthen the decision process, get the help of an independent person to identify which decision makers are likely to be affected by self-interest, emotional attachments, or misleading memories.

Example: The about-to-be-promoted head of the cosmetics business at one Indian company was considering whether to appoint her number two as her successor. She recognized that her judgment might be distorted by her attachment to her colleague and by her vested interest in keeping her workload down during her transition. The executive asked a headhunter to evaluate her colleague and to determine whether better candidates could be found externally.

If the risk of distorted decision making is high, companies need to build safeguards into the decision process: Expose decision makers to additional experience and analysis, design in more debate and opportunities for challenge, and add more oversight.

Example: In helping the CEO make an important strategic decision, the chairman of one global chemical company encouraged the chief executive to seek advice from investment bankers, set up a project team to analyze options, and create a steering committee that included the chairman and the CFO to generate the decision.

high-quality move in as little as six seconds by drawing on patterns he or she has seen before. But pattern recognition can also mislead us. When we're dealing with seemingly familiar situations, our brains can cause us to think we understand them when we don't.

What happened to Matthew Broderick during Hurricane Katrina is instructive. Broderick had been involved in operations centers in Vietnam and in other military engagements, and he had led the Homeland Security Operations Center during previous hurricanes. These experiences had taught him that early reports surrounding a major event are often false: It's better to wait for the "ground truth" from a reliable source before acting. Unfortunately, he had no experience with a hurricane hitting a city built below sea level.

By late on August 29, some 12 hours after Katrina hit New Orleans, Broderick had received 17 reports of major flooding and levee breaches. But he also had gotten conflicting information. The Army Corps of Engineers had reported that it had no evidence of levee breaches, and a late afternoon CNN report from Bourbon Street in the French Quarter had shown city dwellers partying and claiming they had dodged the bullet. Broderick's pattern-recognition process told him that these contrary reports were the ground truth he was looking for. So before going home for the night, he issued a situation report stating that the levees had not been breached, although he did add that further assessment would be needed the next day.

Emotional tagging is the process by which emotional information attaches itself to the thoughts and experiences stored in our memories. This emotional information tells us whether to pay attention to something or not, and it tells us what sort of action we should be contemplating (immediate or postponed, fight or flight). When the parts of our brains controlling emotions are damaged, we can see how important emotional tagging is: Neurological research shows that we become slow and incompetent decision makers even though we can retain the capacity for objective analysis.

Like pattern recognition, emotional tagging helps us reach sensible decisions most of the time. But it, too, can mislead us. Take the case of Wang Laboratories, the top company in the word-processing industry in the early 1980s. Recognizing that his company's future was threatened by the rise of the personal computer, founder An Wang built a machine to compete in this sector. Unfortunately, he chose to create a proprietary operating system despite the fact that the IBM PC was clearly becoming the dominant standard in the industry. This blunder, which contributed to Wang's demise a few years later, was heavily influenced by An Wang's dislike of IBM. He believed he had been cheated by IBM over a new technology he had invented early in his career. These feelings made him reject a software platform linked to an IBM product even though the platform was provided by a third party, Microsoft.

Why doesn't the brain pick up on such errors and correct them? The most obvious reason is that much of the mental work we do is unconscious. This makes it hard to check the data and logic we use when we make a decision. Typically, we spot bugs in our personal software only when we see the results of our errors in judgment. Matthew Broderick found out that his ground-truth rule of thumb was an inappropriate response to Hurricane Katrina only after it was too late. An Wang found out that his preference for proprietary software was flawed only after Wang's personal computer failed in the market.

Compounding the problem of high levels of unconscious thinking is the lack of checks and balances in our decision making. Our brains do not naturally follow the classical textbook model: Lay out the options, define the objectives, and assess each option against each objective. Instead, we analyze the situation using pattern recognition and arrive at a decision to act or not by using emotional tags. The two processes happen almost instantaneously. Indeed, as the research of psychologist Gary Klein shows, our brains leap to conclusions and are reluctant to consider alternatives. Moreover, we are particularly bad at revisiting our initial assessment of a situation—our initial frame.

An exercise we frequently run at Ashridge Business School shows how hard it is to challenge the initial frame. We give students a case that presents a new technology as a good business opportunity. Often, a team works many hours before it challenges this frame and starts, correctly, to see the new technology as a major threat to the company's dominant market position. Even though the financial model consistently calculates negative returns from launching the new technology, some teams never challenge their original frame and end up proposing aggressive investments.

Raising the Red Flag

In analyzing how it is that good leaders made bad judgments, we found they were affected in all cases by three factors that either distorted their emotional tags or encouraged them to see a false pattern. We call these factors "red flag conditions."

The first and most familiar red flag condition, *the presence of inappropriate self-interest,* typically biases the emotional importance we place on information, which in turn makes us readier to perceive the patterns we want to see. Research has shown that even well-intentioned professionals, such as doctors and auditors, are unable to prevent self-interest from biasing their judgments of which medicine to prescribe or opinion to give during an audit.

The second, somewhat less familiar condition is *the presence of distorting attachments.* We can become attached to people, places, and things, and these bonds can affect the judgments we form about both the situation we face and the appropriate actions to take. The reluctance executives often feel to sell a unit they've worked in nicely captures the power of inappropriate attachments.

The final red flag condition is *the presence of misleading memories.* These are memories that seem relevant and comparable to the current situation but lead our thinking down the wrong path. They can cause us to overlook or undervalue some important differentiating factors, as Matthew Broderick did when he gave too little thought to the implications of a hurricane hitting a city below sea level. The chance of being misled by memories is intensified by any emotional tags we have attached to the past experience. If our decisions in the previous similar experience worked well, we'll be all the more likely to overlook key differences.

That's what happened to William Smithburg, former chairman of Quaker Oats. He acquired Snapple because of his vivid memories of Gatorade, Quaker's most successful deal. Snapple, like Gatorade, appeared to be a new drinks company that could be improved with Quaker's marketing and management skills. Unfortunately, the similarities between Snapple and Gatorade proved to be superficial, which meant that Quaker ended up destroying rather than creating value. In fact, Snapple was Smithburg's worst deal.

Of course, part of what we are saying is common knowledge: People have biases, and it's important to manage decisions so that these biases balance out. Many experienced leaders do this already. But we're arguing here that, given the way the brain works, we cannot rely on leaders to spot and safeguard against their own errors in judgment. For important decisions, we need a deliberate, structured way to identify likely sources of bias—those red flag conditions—and we need to strengthen the group decision-making process.

Consider the situation faced by Rita Chakra, head of the cosmetics business of Choudry Holdings (the names of the companies and people cited in this and the following examples have been disguised). She was promoted head of the consumer products division and needed to decide whether to promote her number two into her cosmetics job or recruit someone from outside. Can we anticipate any potential red flags in this decision? Yes, her emotional tags could be unreliable because of a distorting attachment she may have to her colleague or an inappropriate self-interest she could have in keeping her workload down while changing jobs. Of course we don't know for certain whether Rita feels this attachment or holds that vested interest. And since the greater part of decision making is unconscious, Rita would not know either. What we do know is that there is a risk. So how should Rita protect herself, or how should her boss help her protect herself?

The simple answer is to involve someone else—someone who has no inappropriate attachments or self-interest. This could be Rita's boss, the head of human resources, a headhunter, or a trusted colleague. That person could challenge her thinking, force her to review her logic, encourage her to consider options, and possibly even champion a solution she would find uncomfortable. Fortunately, in this situation, Rita was already aware of some red flag conditions, and so she involved a headhunter to help her evaluate her colleague and external candidates. In the end, Rita did appoint her colleague but only after checking to see if her judgment was biased.

We've found many leaders who intuitively understand that their thinking or their colleagues' thinking can be distorted. But few leaders do so in a structured way, and as a result many fail to provide sufficient safeguards against bad decisions. Let's look now at a couple of companies that approached the problem of decision bias systematically by recognizing and reducing the risk posed by red flag conditions.

Safeguarding Against Your Biases

A European multinational we'll call Global Chemicals had an underperforming division. The management team in charge of the division had twice promised a turnaround and twice failed to deliver. The CEO, Mark Thaysen, was weighing his options.

This division was part of Thaysen's growth strategy. It had been assembled over the previous five years through two large and four smaller acquisitions. Thaysen had led the two larger acquisitions and appointed the managers who were struggling to perform. The chairman of the supervisory board, Olaf Grunweld, decided to consider whether Thaysen's judgment about the underperforming division might be biased and, if so, how he might help. Grunweld was not second-guessing Thaysen's thinking. He was merely alert to the possibility that the CEO's views might be distorted.

Grunweld started by looking for red flag conditions. (For a description of a process for identifying red flags, see the sidebar, "Identifying Red Flags.") Thaysen built the underperforming division, and his attachment to it might have made him reluctant to abandon the strategy or the team he had put in place. What's more, because in the past he had successfully supported the local managers during a tough turnaround in another division, Thaysen ran the risk of seeing the wrong pattern and unconsciously favoring the view that continued

Identifying Red Flags

RED FLAGS ARE USEFUL ONLY if they can be spotted before a decision is made. How can you recognize them in complex situations? We have developed the following seven-step process:

1. **Lay out the range of options.** It's never possible to list them all. But it's normally helpful to note the extremes. These provide boundaries for the decision.

2. **List the main decision makers.** Who is going to be influential in making the judgment calls and the final choice? There may be only one or two people involved. But there could also be 10 or more.

3. **Choose one decision maker to focus on.** It's usually best to start with the most influential person. Then identify red flag conditions that might distort that individual's thinking.

4. **Check for inappropriate self-interest or distorting attachments.** Is any option likely to be particularly attractive or unattractive to the decision maker because of personal interests or attachments to people, places, or things?

---

support was needed in this situation, too. Thus alerted to Thaysen's possible distorting attachments and potential misleading memories, Grunweld considered three types of safeguards to strengthen the decision process.

Injecting Fresh Experience or Analysis
You can often counteract biases by exposing the decision maker to new information and a different take on the problem. In this instance, Grunweld asked an investment bank to tell Thaysen what value the company

Do any of these interests or attachments conflict with the objectives of the main stakeholders?

5. **Check for misleading memories.** What are the uncertainties in this decision? For each area of uncertainty, consider whether the decision maker might draw on potentially misleading memories. Think about past experiences that could mislead, especially ones with strong emotional associations. Think also about previous judgments that could now be unsound, given the current situation.

6. **Repeat the analysis with the next most influential person.** In a complex case, it may be necessary to consider many more people, and the process may bring to light a long list of possible red flags.

7. **Review the list of red flags you have identified** and determine whether the brain's normally efficient pattern-recognition and emotional-tagging processes might be biased in favor of or against some options. If so, put one or more safeguards in place.

might get from selling the underperforming division. Grunweld felt this would encourage Thaysen to at least consider that radical option—a step Thaysen might too quickly dismiss if he had become overly attached to the unit or its management team.

Introducing Further Debate and Challenge
This safeguard can ensure that biases are confronted explicitly. It works best when the power structure of the group debating the issue is balanced. While Thaysen's chief financial officer was a strong individual,

Grunweld felt that the other members of the executive group would be likely to follow Thaysen's lead without challenging him. Moreover, the head of the underperforming division was a member of the executive group, making it hard for open debate to occur. So Grunweld proposed a steering committee consisting of himself, Thaysen, and the CFO. Even if Thaysen strongly pushed for a particular solution, Grunweld and the CFO would make sure his reasoning was properly challenged and debated. Grunweld also suggested that Thaysen set up a small project team, led by the head of strategy, to analyze all the options and present them to the steering committee.

Imposing Stronger Governance

The requirement that a decision be ratified at a higher level provides a final safeguard. Stronger governance does not eliminate distorted thinking, but it can prevent distortions from leading to a bad outcome. At Global Chemicals, the governance layer was the supervisory board. Grunweld realized, however, that its objectivity could be compromised because he was a member of both the board and the steering committee. So he asked two of his board colleagues to be ready to argue against the proposal emanating from the steering committee if they felt uncomfortable.

In the end, the steering committee proposed an outright sale of the division, a decision the board approved. The price received was well above expectations, convincing all that they had chosen the best option.

The chairman of Global Chemicals took the lead role in designing the decision process. That was appropriate given the importance of the decision. But many decisions are made at the operating level, where direct CEO involvement is neither feasible nor desirable. That was the case at Southern Electricity, a division of a larger U.S. utility. Southern consisted of three operating units and two powerful functions. Recent regulatory changes meant that prices could not be raised and might even fall. So managers were looking for ways to cut back on capital expenditures.

Division head Jack Williams recognized that the managers were also risk averse, preferring to replace equipment early with the best upgrades available. This, he realized, was a result of some high-profile breakdowns in the past, which had exposed individuals both to complaints from customers and to criticism from colleagues. Williams believed the emotional tags associated with these experiences might be distorting their judgment.

What could he do to counteract these effects? Williams rejected the idea of stronger governance; he felt that neither his management team nor the parent company's executives knew enough to do the job credibly. He also rejected additional analysis, because Southern's analysis was already rigorous. He concluded that he had to find a way to inject more debate into the decision process and enable people who understood the details to challenge the thinking.

His first thought was to involve himself and his head of finance in the debates, but he didn't have time to

consider the merits of hundreds of projects, and he did-
n't understand the details well enough to effectively
challenge decisions earlier in the process than he currently was doing, at the final approval stage. Williams
finally decided to get the unit and function heads to
challenge one another, facilitated by a consultant.
Rather than impose this process on his managers,
Williams chose to share his thinking with them. Using
the language of red flags, he was able to get them to see
the problem without their feeling threatened. The new
approach was very successful. The reduced capital-
expenditure target was met with room to spare and
without Williams having to make any of the tough judgment calls himself.

———————

Because we now understand more about how the brain
works, we can anticipate the circumstances in which errors of judgment may occur and guard against them. So
rather than rely on the wisdom of experienced chair-
men, the humility of CEOs, or the standard organizational checks and balances, we urge all involved in
important decisions to explicitly consider whether red
flags exist and, if they do, to lobby for appropriate safeguards. Decisions that involve no red flags need many
fewer checks and balances and thus less bureaucracy.
Some of those resources could then be devoted to pro-
tecting the decisions most at risk with more intrusive
and robust protections.

ANDREW CAMPBELL and **JO WHITEHEAD** are directors of Ashridge Strategic Management Centre in London. **SYDNEY FINKELSTEIN** is the Steven Roth Professor of Management at Dartmouth's Tuck School of Business. All three are coauthors of *Think Again: Why Good Leaders Make Bad Decisions and How to Keep It from Happening to You* (Harvard Business Review Press, 2009).

Originally published in February 2009. Reprint R0902D

Stop Making Plans; Start Making Decisions

by Michael C. Mankins and Richard Steele

IS STRATEGIC PLANNING COMPLETELY USELESS? That was the question the CEO of a global manufacturer recently asked himself. Two years earlier, he had launched an ambitious overhaul of the company's planning process. The old approach, which required business-unit heads to make regular presentations to the firm's executive committee, had broken down entirely. The ExCom members—the CEO, COO, CFO, CTO, and head of HR—had grown tired of sitting through endless PowerPoint presentations that provided them few opportunities to challenge the business units' assumptions or influence their strategies. And the unit heads had complained that the ExCom reviews were long on exhortation but short on executable advice. Worse, the reviews led to very few worthwhile decisions.

The revamped process incorporated state-of-the-art thinking about strategic planning. To avoid information overload, it limited each business to 15 "high-impact" exhibits describing the unit's strategy. To ensure thoughtful discussions, it required that all presentations and supporting materials be distributed to the ExCom at least a week in advance. The review sessions themselves were restructured to allow ample time for give-and-take between the corporate team and the business-unit executives. And rather than force the unit heads to traipse off to headquarters for meetings, the ExCom agreed to spend an unprecedented six weeks each spring visiting all 22 units for daylong sessions. The intent was to make the strategy reviews longer, more focused, and more consequential.

It didn't work. After using the new process for two planning cycles, the CEO gathered feedback from the participants through an anonymous survey. To his dismay, the report contained a litany of complaints: "It takes too much time." "It's at too high a level." "It's disconnected from the way we run the business." And so on. Most damning of all, however, was the respondents' near-universal view that the new approach produced very few real decisions. The CEO was dumbfounded. How could the company's cutting-edge planning process still be so badly broken? More important, what should he do to make strategic planning drive more, better, and faster decisions?

Like this CEO, many executives have grown skeptical of strategic planning. Is it any wonder? Despite all the time and energy most companies put into strategic planning, the process is most often a barrier to good decision making, our research indicates. As a result,

Idea in Brief

Most executives view traditional strategic planning as worthless. Why? The process contains serious flaws. First, it's conducted annually, so it doesn't help executives respond swiftly to threats and opportunities (a new competitor, a possible acquisition) that crop up throughout the year.

Second, it unfolds unit by unit—with executive committee members visiting one unit at a time to review their strategic plans. Executives lack sufficient information to provide worthwhile guidance during these "business tours." And the visits take them away from urgent companywide issues, such as whether to enter a new market, outsource a function, or restructure the organization.

Frustrated by these constraints, executives routinely sidestep their company's formal strategic planning process—making ad hoc decisions based on scanty analysis and meager debate. Result? Decisions made incorrectly, too slowly, or not at all.

How to improve the quality *and* quantity of your strategic decisions? Use **continuous issues-focused strategic planning**. Throughout the year, identify the issues you must resolve to enhance your company's performance—particularly those spanning multiple business units. Debate one issue at a time until you've reached a decision. And add issues to your agenda as business realities change.

Your reward? More rigorous debate and more significant strategic decisions each year—made precisely when they're needed.

strategic planning doesn't really influence most companies' strategy.

In the following pages, we will demonstrate that the failure of most strategic planning is due to two factors: It is typically an annual process, and it is most often focused on individual business units. As such, the process is completely at odds with the way executives actually make important strategy decisions, which are

Idea in Practice

To create an effective strategic-planning process:

Link Decision Making and Planning. Create a mechanism that helps you identify the decisions you *must* make to create more shareholder value. Once you've made those decisions, use your traditional planning process to develop an implementation road map.

> *Example:* At Boeing Commercial Airplanes, executives meet regularly to uncover the company's most pressing, long-term strategic issues (such as evolving product strategy, or fueling growth in services). Upon selecting a course of action, they update their long-range business plan with an implementation strategy for that decision. (By separating—but linking—planning and execution,

Boeing makes faster and better decisions.)

Focus on Companywide Issues. During strategy discussions, focus on issues spanning multiple business units.

> *Example:* Facing a shortage of investment ideas, Microsoft's leaders began defining issues—such as PC market growth and security—that are critical throughout the company. Dialogues between unit leaders and the executive committee now focus on what Microsoft as a whole can do to address each issue—not which strategies individual units should formulate. Countless new growth opportunities have surfaced.

Develop Strategy Continuously. Spread strategy reviews throughout the year

neither constrained by the calendar nor defined by unit boundaries. Not surprisingly, then, senior executives routinely sidestep the planning process. They make the decisions that really shape their company's strategy and determine its future—decisions about mergers and acquisitions, product launches, corporate restructurings, and the like—outside the planning process, rather than squeezing them into a two- or three-month window. You'll be able to focus on—and resolve—one issue at a time. And you'll have the flexibility to add issues as soon as business conditions change.

Example: Executives at multi-industry giant Textron review two to three units' strategy per quarter rather than compressing all unit reviews into one quarter annually. They also hold continuous reviews designed to address each strategic issue on the company's agenda. Once an also-ran among its peers, Textron was a top-quartile performer during 2004–2005.

Structure Strategy Reviews to Produce Results. Design and conduct strategy sessions so that participants agree on facts related to each issue before proposing solutions.

Example: At Textron, each strategic issue is resolved through a disciplined process: In one session, the management committee debates the issue at hand and reaches agreement on the relevant facts (e.g., customers' purchase behaviors, a key market's profitability figures). The group then generates several viable strategy alternatives. In a second session, the committee evaluates the alternatives from a strategic and financial perspective and selects a course of action. By moving from facts to alternatives to choices, the group reaches many more decisions than before.

typically in an ad hoc fashion, without rigorous analysis or productive debate. Critical decisions are made incorrectly or not at all. More than anything else, this disconnect—between the way planning works and the way decision making happens—explains the frustration, if not outright antipathy, most executives feel toward strategic planning.

But companies can fix the process if they attack its root problems. A small number of forward-looking companies have thrown out their calendar-driven, business-unit-focused planning processes and replaced them with continuous, issues-focused decision making. By changing the timing and focus of strategic planning, they've also changed the nature of top management's discussions about strategy—from "review and approve" to "debate and decide," meaning that senior executives seriously think through every major decision and its implications for the company's performance and value. Indeed, these companies use the strategy development process to drive decision making. As a consequence, they make more than twice as many important strategic decisions each year as companies that follow the traditional planning model. (See the sidebar "Who Makes More Decisions?") These companies have stopped making plans and started making decisions.

Where Planning Goes Wrong

In the fall of 2005, Marakon Associates, in collaboration with the Economist Intelligence Unit, surveyed senior executives from 156 large companies worldwide, all with sales of $1 billion or more (40% of them had revenues over $10 billion). We asked these executives how their companies developed long-range plans and how effectively they thought their planning processes drove strategic decisions.

The results of the survey confirmed what we have observed over many years of consulting: The timing

Who Makes More Decisions?

COMPANIES SEE A DRAMATIC INCREASE in the quality of their decision making once they abandon the traditional planning model, which is calendar driven and focused on the business units. In our survey, the companies that broke most completely with the past made more than twice as many strategic decisions each year as companies wedded to tradition. What's more, the new structure of the planning process ensures that the decisions are probably the best that could have been made, given the information available to managers at the time.

Here are the average numbers of major strategic decisions reached per year in companies that take the following approaches to strategic planning:

Annual review focused on business units

2.5 decisions per year

Annual review focused on issues

3.5 decisions per year

Continuous review focused on business units

4.1 decisions per year

Continuous review focused on issues

6.1 decisions per year

Source: Marakon Associates and the Economist Intelligence Unit

and structure of strategic planning are obstacles to good decision making. Specifically, we found that companies with standard planning processes and practices make only 2.5 major strategic decisions each year, on average (by "major," we mean they have the potential to increase company profits by 10% or more over the long term). It's hard to imagine that with so few strategic decisions driving growth, these companies can keep moving forward and deliver the financial performance that investors expect.

Even worse, we suspect that the few decisions companies do reach are made in spite of the strategic planning process, not because of it. Indeed, the traditional planning model is so cumbersome and out of sync with the way executives want and need to make decisions that top managers all too often sidestep the process when making their biggest strategic choices.

With the big decisions being made outside the planning process, strategic planning becomes merely a codification of judgments top management has already made, rather than a vehicle for identifying and debating the critical decisions that the company needs to make to produce superior performance. Over time, managers begin to question the value of strategic planning, withdraw from it, and come to rely on other processes for setting company strategy.

The Calendar Effect

At 66% of the companies in our survey, planning is a periodic event, often conducted as a precursor to the yearly budgeting and capital-approval processes. In fact, linking strategic planning to these other management processes is often cited as a best practice. But forcing strategic planning into an annual cycle risks making it irrelevant to executives, who must make many important decisions throughout the year.

There are two major drawbacks to such a rigid schedule. The first might be called the *time* problem.

A once-a-year planning schedule simply does not give executives sufficient time to address the issues that most affect performance. According to our survey, companies that follow an annual planning calendar devote less than nine weeks per year to strategy development. That's barely two months to collect relevant facts, set strategic priorities, weigh competing alternatives, and make important strategic choices. Many issues—particularly those spanning multiple businesses, crossing geographic boundaries, or involving entire value chains—cannot be resolved effectively in such a short time. It took Boeing, for example, almost two years to decide to outsource major activities such as wing manufacturing.

Constrained by the planning calendar, corporate executives face two choices: They can either not address these complex issues—in effect, throwing them in the "too-hard" bucket—or they can address them through some process other than strategic planning. In both cases, strategic planning is marginalized and separated from strategic decision making.

Then there's the *timing* problem. Even when executives allot sufficient time in strategy development to address tough issues, the timing of the process can create problems. At most companies, strategic planning is a batch process in which managers analyze market and competitor information, identify threats and opportunities, and then define a multiyear plan. But in the real world, managers make strategic decisions continuously, often motivated by an immediate need for action (or reaction). When a new competitor enters a market, for instance, or a rival introduces a new technology, executives must act quickly and decisively to safeguard the company's performance. But very few companies (less than 10%, according to our survey) have any sort of rigorous or disciplined process for responding to changes in the external environment. Instead, managers rely on ad hoc processes to correct course or make opportunistic moves. Once again, strategic planning is sidelined, and executives risk making poor decisions that have not been carefully thought through.

M&A decisions provide a particularly egregious example of the timing problem. Acquisition opportunities tend to emerge spontaneously, the result of changes in management at a target company, the actions of a competitor, or some other unpredictable event. Faced with a promising opportunity and limited time in which to act, executives can't wait until the opportunity is evaluated as part of the next annual planning cycle, so they assess the deal and make a quick decision. But because there's often no proper review process, the softer customer- and people-related issues so critical to effective integration of an acquired company can get shortchanged. It is no coincidence that failure to plan for integration is often cited as the primary cause of deal failure.

The Business-Unit Effect

The organizational focus of the typical planning process compounds its calendar effects—or, perhaps more aptly, defects. Two-thirds of the executives we surveyed indicated that strategic planning at their companies is conducted business by business—that is, it is focused on units or groups of units. But 70% of the senior executives who responded to our survey stated they make decisions issue by issue. For example, should we enter China? Should we outsource manufacturing? Should we acquire our distributor? Given this mismatch between the way planning is organized and the way big decisions are made, it's hardly surprising that, once again, corporate leaders look elsewhere for guidance and inspiration. In fact, only 11% of the executives we surveyed believed strongly that planning was worth the effort.

The organizational focus of traditional strategic planning also creates distance, even antagonism, between corporate executives and business-unit managers. Consider, for example, the way most companies conduct strategy reviews—as formal meetings between senior managers and the heads of each business unit. While these reviews are intended to produce a fact-based dialogue, they often amount to little more than business tourism. The executive committee flies in for a day, sees the sights, meets the natives, and flies out. The business unit, for its part, puts in a lot of work preparing for this royal visit and is keen to make it smooth and trouble free. The unit hopes to escape with few unanswered questions and an approved plan. Accordingly, local managers control the flow of information upward, and senior managers are presented only with information that shows each unit in the best possible light. Opportunities are highlighted; threats are downplayed or omitted.

Even if there's no subterfuge, senior corporate managers still have trouble engaging in constructive dialogue

Traditional Planning

COMPANIES THAT FOLLOW THE TRADITIONAL strategic planning model develop a strategy plan for each business unit at some point during the year. A cross-functional team dedicates less than nine weeks to developing the unit's plan. The executive committee reviews each plan—typically in daylong, on-site meetings—and rubber-stamps the results. The plans are consolidated to produce a companywide strategic plan for review by the board of directors.

Once the strategic-planning cycle is complete, the units dedicate another eight to nine weeks to budgeting and capital planning (in most companies, these processes are not explicitly linked to strategic planning).

The executive committee then holds another round of meetings with each of the business units to negotiate performance targets, resource commitments, and (in many cases) compensation for managers.

The results: an approved but potentially unrealistic strategic plan for each business unit and a separate budget for each unit that is decoupled from the unit's strategic plan.

and debate because of what might be called information asymmetry. They just don't have the information they need to be helpful in guiding business units. So when they're presented with a strategic plan that's too good to be believed, they have only two real options: either reject it—a move that's all but unheard-of at most large companies—or play along and impose stretch targets to secure at least the promise that the unit will improve performance. In both cases, the review does little to drive decisions on issues. It's hardly surprising that only 13% of the executives we surveyed felt that top managers were effectively engaged in all aspects of strategy development at their companies—from target setting to debating alternatives to approving strategies and allocating resources.

Decision-Focused Strategic Planning

Strategic planning can't have impact if it doesn't drive decision making. And it can't drive decision making as long as it remains focused on individual business units and limited by the calendar. Over the past several years, we have observed that many of the best-performing companies have abandoned the traditional approach and are focusing explicitly on reaching decisions through the continuous identification and systematic resolution of strategic issues. (The sidebar "Continuous, Decision-Oriented Planning" presents a detailed example of the issues-oriented approach.) Although these companies have found different specific solutions, all have made essentially the same fundamental changes to their planning and strategy development processes in order to produce more, better, and faster decisions.

They Separate—But Integrate—Decision Making and Plan Making

First and most important, a company must take decisions out of the traditional planning process and create a different, parallel process for developing strategy that helps executives identify the decisions they *need to make* to create more shareholder value over time. The output of this new process isn't a plan at all—it's a set of

Continuous, Decision-Oriented Planning

ONCE THE COMPANY AS A whole has identified its most important strategic priorities (typically in an annual strategy update), executive committee dialogues, spread throughout the year, are set up to reach decisions on as many issues as possible. Since issues frequently span multiple business units, task forces are established to prepare the strategic and financial information that's needed to uncover and evaluate strategy alternatives for each issue. Preparation time may exceed nine weeks. The executive committee engages in two dialogues for each issue at three to four hours each. The first dialogue focuses on reaching agreement on the facts surrounding the issue and on a set of viable alternatives. The second focuses on the evaluation of those alternatives and the selection of the best course of action. Once an issue is resolved, a new one is added to the agenda. Critical issues can be inserted into the planning process at any time as market and competitive conditions change.

Once a decision has been reached, the budgets and capital plans for the affected business units are updated to reflect the selected option. Consequently, the strategic-planning process and the capital and budgeting processes are integrated. This significantly

concrete decisions that management can codify into future business plans through the existing planning process, which remains in place. Identifying and making decisions is distinct from creating, monitoring, and updating a strategic plan, and the two sets of tasks require very different, but integrated, processes.

Boeing Commercial Airplanes (BCA) is a case in point. This business unit, Boeing's largest, has had a long-range business plan (LRBP) process for many years. The reduces the need for lengthy negotiations between the executive committee and unit management over the budget and capital plan.

The results: a concrete plan for addressing each key issue; for each business unit, a continuously updated budget and capital plan that is linked directly to the resolution of critical strategic issues; and more, faster, better decisions per year.

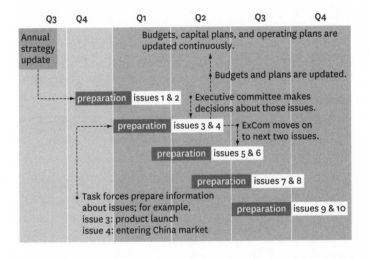

protracted cycles of commercial aircraft production require the unit's CEO, Alan Mulally, and his leadership team to take a long-term view of the business. Accordingly, the unit's LRBP contains a ten-year financial forecast, including projected revenues, backlogs, operating margins, and capital investments. BCA's leadership team reviews the business plan weekly to track the division's performance relative to the plan and to keep the organization focused on execution.

The weekly reviews were invaluable as a performance-monitoring tool at BCA, but they were not particularly effective at bringing new issues to the surface or driving strategic decision making. So in 2001, the unit's leadership team introduced a Strategy Integration Process focused on uncovering and addressing the business's most important strategic issues (such as determining the best go-to-market strategy for the business, driving the evolution of BCA's product strategy, or fueling growth in services). The team assigned to this process holds strategy integration meetings every Monday to track BCA's progress in resolving these long-term issues. Once a specific course of action is agreed upon and approved by BCA's leadership team, the long-range business plan is updated at the next weekly review to reflect the projected change in financial performance.

The time invested in the new decision-making process is more than compensated for by the time saved in the LRBP process, which is now solely focused on strategy execution. The company gets the best of both worlds—disciplined decision making and superior execution. BCA has maintained the value of the LRBP as an execution tool even as it has increased the quality and quantity of important decisions. Managers believe that the new process is at least partially responsible for the sharp turnaround in Boeing's performance since 2001.

They Focus On a Few Key Themes

High-performing companies typically focus their strategy discussions on a limited number of important issues or themes, many of which span multiple businesses.

Moving away from a business-by-business planning model in this way has proved particularly helpful for large, complex organizations, where strategy discussions can quickly get bogged down as each division manager attempts to cover every aspect of the unit's strategy. Business-unit managers should remain involved in corporate-level strategy planning that affects their units. But a focus on issues rather than business units better aligns strategy development with decision making and investment.

Consider Microsoft. The world's leading software maker is a highly matrixed organization. No strategy can be effectively executed at the company without careful coordination across multiple functions and across two or more of Microsoft's seven business units, or, as executives refer to them, "P&Ls"—Client; Server and Tools; Information Worker; MSN; Microsoft Business Solutions; Mobile and Embedded Devices; and Home and Entertainment. In late 2004, faced with a perceived shortage of good investment ideas, CEO Steve Ballmer asked Robert Uhlaner, Microsoft's corporate vice president of strategy, planning, and analysis, to devise a new strategic planning process for the company. Uhlaner put in place a Growth and Performance Planning Process that starts with agreement by Ballmer's leadership team on a set of strategic themes—major issues like PC market growth, the entertainment market, and security—that cross business-unit boundaries. These themes not only frame the dialogue for Microsoft's annual strategy review, they also guide the units in fleshing out investment alternatives to fuel the company's growth.

The Disconnect Between Planning and Decision Making

How Executives Plan

66% periodically

Percentage of surveyed executives saying their companies conduct strategic planning only at prescribed times

67% unit by unit

Percentage saying planning is done unit by unit

How Executives Decide

100% continuously

Percentage of executives saying strategic decisions are made without regard to the calendar

70% issue by issue

Percentage saying decisions are made issue by issue

No wonder only 11% of executives are highly satisfied that strategic planning is worth the effort.

Dialogues between the P&L leaders and Ballmer's team focus on what the company can do to address each strategic theme, rather than on individual unit strategies. The early results of this new process are promising. "You have to be careful what you wish for," Uhlaner says. "Our new process has surfaced countless new opportunities for growth. We no longer worry about a dearth of investment ideas, but how best to fund them."

Like Microsoft, Diageo North America—a division of the international beer, wine, and spirits marketer—has recently changed the way it conducts strategic planning to allocate resources across its diverse portfolio. Diageo historically focused its planning efforts on individual brands. Brand managers were allowed to make the case for additional investment, no matter what the size of the brand or its strategic role in the portfolio. As a result, resource allocation was bedeviled by endless negotiations between the brands and corporate management. This political wrangling made it extremely difficult for Diageo's senior managers to establish a consistent approach to growth, because a lack of transparency prevented them from discerning, from the many requests for additional funding, which brands really deserved more resources and which did not.

Starting in 2001, Diageo overhauled its approach to strategy development. A crucial change was to focus planning on the factors that the company believed would most drive market growth—for example, an increase in the U.S. Hispanic population. By modeling the impact of these factors on the brand portfolio, Diageo has been better able to match its resources with the brands that have the most growth potential so that it can specify the strategies and investments each brand manager should develop, says Jim Moseley, senior vice president of consumer planning and research for Diageo North America. For example, the division now identifies certain brands for growth and earmarks specific resources for investment in these units. This focused approach has enabled the company to shorten the brand planning process and reduce the time spent on negotiations between the brands and division management. It has also given senior management greater confidence in each brand's ability to contribute to Diageo's growth.

They Make Strategy Development Continuous

Effective strategy planners spread strategy reviews throughout the year rather than squeeze them into a two- or three-month window. This allows senior executives to focus on one issue at a time until they reach a decision or set of decisions. Moreover, managers can add issues to the agenda as market and competitive conditions change, so there's no need for ad hoc processes. Senior executives can thus rely on a single strategic planning process—or, perhaps more aptly, a single strategic decision-making model—to drive decision making across the company.

Textron, a $10 billion multi-industry company, has implemented a new, continuous strategy-development process built around a prioritized "decision agenda" comprising the company's most important issues and opportunities. Until 2004, Textron had a fairly traditional strategic planning process. Each spring, the company's operating units—businesses as diverse as Bell Helicopter, E-Z-Go golf cars, and Jacobsen turf maintenance equipment—would develop a five-year strategic plan based on standard templates. Unit managers would then review their strategic plans with Textron's management committee (the company's top five executives) during daylong sessions at each unit. Once the strategy reviews were complete, the units incorporated the results, as best they could, into their annual operating plans and capital budgets.

In June 2004, dissatisfied with the quality and pace of the decision making that resulted from the company's strategy reviews, CEO Lewis Campbell asked Stuart Grief, Textron's vice president for strategy and business development, to rethink the company's strategic planning process. After carefully reviewing the company's practices and gathering feedback from its 30 top executives, Grief and his team designed a new Textron Strategy Process.

There were two important changes. First, rather than concentrate all of the operating-unit strategy reviews in the second quarter of each year, the company now spreads strategy dialogues throughout the year—two to three units are reviewed per quarter. Second, rather than organize the management committee dialogues around business-unit plans, Textron now holds continuous reviews that are designed to address each strategic issue on the company's decision agenda. Both changes have enabled Textron's management committee to be much more effectively engaged in business-unit strategy development. The changes have also ensured that there's a forum in which cross-unit issues can be raised and addressed by top management, with input from relevant business-unit managers. The process has significantly increased the number of strategic decisions the company makes each year. As a result, Textron has gone from being an also-ran among its multi-industrial peers to a top-quartile performer over the past 18 months.

John Cullivan, the director of strategy at Cardinal Health, one of the world's leading health-care products and services companies, reports similar benefits from shifting to a continuous planning model. "Continuous decision making is tough to establish because it requires the reallocation of management time at the top levels of the company," he says. "But the process has enabled us to get sharper focus on the short-term performance of our vertical businesses and make faster progress on our longer-term priorities, some of which are horizontal opportunities that cut across businesses and thus are difficult to manage."

To facilitate continuous strategic decision making, Cardinal has made a series of important changes to its traditional planning process. At the corporate level, for example, the company has put in place a rolling six-month agenda for its executive committee dialogues, a practice that allows everyone inside Cardinal to know what issues management is working on and when decisions will be reached. Similar decision agendas are used at the business-unit and functional levels, ensuring that common standards are applied to all important decisions at the company. And to support continuous decision making at Cardinal, the company has trained "black belts" in new analytical tools and processes and deployed them throughout the organization. This provides each of the company's businesses and functions with the resources needed to address strategic priorities that emerge over time.

They Structure Strategy Reviews to Produce Real Decisions

The most common obstacles to decision making at large companies are disagreements among executives over past decisions, current alternatives, and even the facts presented to support strategic plans. Leading companies structure their strategy review sessions to overcome these problems.

At Textron, for example, strategic-issue reviews are organized around "facts, alternatives, and choices." Each issue is addressed in two half-day sessions with the company's management committee, allowing for eight to ten issues to be resolved throughout the year. In the first session, the management committee debates and reaches agreement on the relevant facts—information on the profitability of key markets, the actions of competitors, the purchase behavior of customers, and so on—and a limited set of viable strategy alternatives. The purpose of this first meeting is not to reach agreement on a specific course of action; rather, the meeting ensures that the group has the best possible information and a robust set of alternatives to consider. The second session is focused on evaluating these alternatives from a strategic and financial perspective and selecting the best course of action. By separating the dialogue around facts and alternatives from the debate over choices, Textron's management committee avoids many of the bottlenecks that plague strategic decision making at most companies and reaches many more decisions than it otherwise would.

Like Textron, Cadbury Schweppes has changed the structure of its strategy dialogues to focus top managers more explicitly on decision making. In 2002, after acquiring and integrating gum-maker Adams—a move that significantly expanded Cadbury's product and geographic reach—the company realized it needed to rethink how it was conducting dialogues about strategy between the corporate center and the businesses. The company made two important changes. First, strategy dialogues were redesigned to incorporate a standard set of facts and metrics about consumers, customers, and competitors. This information helped get critical commercial choices in front of top managers, so that the choices were no longer buried in the business units. Second, senior executives' time was reallocated so they could pay more attention to markets that were crucial to realizing Cadbury's ten-year vision and to making important decisions.

Cadbury's top team now spends one full week per year in each of the countries that are most critical to driving the company's performance, so that important decisions can be informed by direct observation as well as through indirect analysis. Strategy dialogues are now based on a much deeper understanding of the markets. Cadbury's strategic reviews no longer merely consist of reviews of and approval of a strategic plan, and they produce many more important decisions.

Done right, strategic planning can have an enormous impact on a company's performance and long-term value. By creating a planning process that enables managers to discover great numbers of hidden strategic issues and make more decisions, companies will open the door to many more opportunities for long-term growth and profitability. By embracing decision-focused planning, companies will almost certainly find that the quantity and quality of their decisions will improve. And—no co-incidence—they will discover an improvement in the quality of the dialogue between senior corporate managers and unit managers. Corporate executives will gain a better understanding of the challenges their companies face, and unit managers will benefit fully from the experience and insights of the company's leaders. As Mark Reckitt, a director of group strategy at Cadbury Schweppes, puts it: "Continuous, decision-focused strategic planning has helped our top management team to streamline its agenda and work with business units and functional management to make far better business-strategy and commercial decisions."

MICHAEL C. MANKINS is a managing partner in the San Francisco office of Marakon Associates, an international strategy consulting firm. **RICHARD STEELE** is a partner in Marakon's New York office.

Originally published in January 2006. Reprint R0601F

Index

business units
  continuous decision-
    oriented planning and,
    230–231, 233
  decision making by, 136–137,
    148–151, 192–194
  traditional strategic
    planning based in, 219, 223,
    226–229

Cadbury Schweppes, 239–240,
  241
calendar effect, in strategic
  planning, 224–226
Campbell, Andrew, 199–215
Campbell, Lewis, 237
candor, in meetings, 60–61
capital investment, decision
  making on, 136–137
Capital One, 195
capital plans, in strategic
  planning, 230–231
Cardinal Health, 237–238
Caruso, Eugene, 172
Castro, Fidel, 122
Centre for Evidence-Based
  Medicine, 88–89, 103
Charan, Ram, 51–73
Chastain, Brandi, 90–91
Chevron, 105–106, 190–191
Chrysler, 125, 199
Chugh, Dolly, 161–183
Cisco, 87
clarity, about decision making
  role, 143, 152, 156
Cleaver, Harlan, 95
Clinton, Bill, 80
closure
  in decision-making process,
    113, 116, 126–129
  in meetings, 60, 61

cognitive biases
  decision making and. *See*
    traps in decision making
  overoptimism and, 32, 36
cognitive constructive conflict,
  112, 116, 117
collaboration
  decision making and, 151–152
  dialogue encouraging, 61, 64,
    67, 68, 69
  overclaiming credit in, 172
College Board, 33
committees
  decision making and, 150,
    202, 212, 217, 221, 236
  executive, 54, 217, 219, 220,
    227, 228, 230–231, 238
  management, 221, 236,
    237, 239
  planning and, 217, 219, 220,
    221, 227, 228, 230–231, 237,
    238, 239
  steering, 202, 212, 217
compensation, and forced
  ranking ("rank and yank"),
  87, 90–92
compensation reviews, 70
compensation targets, and
  overoptimistic forecasts, 39
competitive advantage
  evidence-based management
    and, 81
  first-mover-advantage myth
    on, 84
competitor neglect, and
  overoptimism, 38
confirming-evidence trap, 13–16
  causes and manifestations of,
    3, 13–15, 26
  guarding against, 15–16
conflict, in decision-making
  process, 111, 112, 115, 116–121

You don't want to miss these...

We've combed through hundreds of *Harvard Business Review* articles on key management topics and selected *the* most important ones to help you maximize your own and your organization's performance.